The Mi
of the

The Mistaken History of the Korean War

What We Got Wrong Then and Now

PAUL M. EDWARDS

McFarland & Company, Inc., Publishers
Jefferson, North Carolina

LIBRARY OF CONGRESS CATALOGUING-IN-PUBLICATION DATA

Names: Edwards, Paul M.
Title: The mistaken history of the Korean War : what we got wrong
    then and now / Paul M. Edwards.
Description: Jefferson, North Carolina : McFarland & Company, Inc.,
    Publishers, 2018. | Includes bibliographical references and index.
Identifiers: LCCN 2018000264 | ISBN 9781476670485 (softcover :
    acid free paper) ∞
Subjects: LCSH: Korean War, 1950–1953. | Korean War, 1950–1953—
    Historiography.
Classification: LCC DS918 .E364 2018 | DDC 951.904/2—dc23
LC record available at https://lccn.loc.gov/2018000264

BRITISH LIBRARY CATALOGUING DATA ARE AVAILABLE

ISBN (print) 978-1-4766-7048-5
ISBN (ebook) 978-1-4766-3077-9

Front cover: Corporal Charles E. Price plays "Taps" at a cemetery
for his fellow Marines in Hungnam, Korea, on December 13, 1950
(Department of Defense)

Printed in the United States of America

McFarland & Company, Inc., Publishers
    Box 611, Jefferson, North Carolina 28640
        www.mcfarlandpub.com

To the life and memory
of Frank Kelly and Robert Kozuki

Table of Contents

Acknowledgments

A special thanks must be expressed to the veterans of the Korean War, and their families, who deposited their papers in archives and depositories across the nation. This is especially true of those gifts given to the Harry S. Truman Presidential Museum and Library and to the Center for the Study of the Korean War in Independence, Missouri, where students and scholars continue to profit from them. These personal papers have been invaluable in this study. For many of those who survived the war in Korea, it remained a private experience, and to expose their letters and memoirs to the public was difficult indeed. While much of the information they provide has been used as available, it is important to note that their ideas, points of view, sometimes their words, as well as their unspoken emotions, have been adopted with great care and respect. The selection of what to use and the interpretations of their meaning are my own and I take full responsibility for them.

Appreciation is also expressed to the many veterans who have shared their views through oral histories in which they talk about memories and why they have been so easily forgotten. It is interesting to note that many of these conversations are different from those provided in less formal discussions and recordings. Those differences have been dependent on notes taken at the time and are identified for documentation. It is important to acknowledge the help of colleagues such as the highly insightful Dr. James Matray, the consummate researcher Dr. Mike Pearlman, and the honestly cautious Dr. Allen Millet for their assistance primarily via the written works. Special thanks are extended to those scholars who have produced highly significant monographs, among these Franklin Cooling's "Allied Interoperability in the Korean War"[1] and a "History of the Korean War: Inter-Allied Cooperation During Combat Operations 1952."[2] Special acknowledgment must go to

Gordon L. Rottman, author of *Korean War Order of Battle: United States, United Nations, and Communist Ground, Naval and Air Forces, 1950–1955*, an invaluable work that was long needed and is now much appreciated.[3]

Thanks also to Melinda L. Pash, a delightful young lady who studied at the Center for the Study of the Korean War, and who has produced in her book *In the Shadow of the Greatest Generation: The Americans Who Fought the Korean War* the first real study of the Korean veteran.

I am indeed thankful as well to the directors and staffs of the many libraries and archive sources I consulted, especially the Truman Presidential Museum and Library, the Eisenhower Presidential Library in Kansas, the Center for the Study of the Korean War in Independence, Missouri, and the Joint Services Command and Staff College Library at Fort Leavenworth, Kansas. As always they have been remarkably helpful. Amazement and special thanks to Dr. Thomas Peterman, whose electronic expertise matched with deep friendship proved so invaluable.

Several individuals remain to be thanked for their time and consideration. These include longtime friends and veterans Frank Kelly, William Walter St. Clair, Robert Kozuki, and Alma Blair. Friends and colleagues Dan Jorgenson, Greg Edwards, Jeanne Earnest, Darian Cobb, Cindy Easter, Lawrence Oglethorpe, Marilu Goodyear, Greg Smith, Paul Wolfgear, Clare Vlahos, and Mike Devine. And, of course, my wife Carolynn Jean, who these many years has always been there.

A Note on Other Nations' Resources

Something needs to be said about the archival and cultural depositories maintained by other nations. This book is about American memories and national misconceptions and makes no effort to acknowledge how the war has been covered by other participating nations. If interested, consult with *United Nations Participants in the Korean War: The Contributions of the 45 Member Countries*.[4] Of those involved, only a small number have created a national history of the event, and there are few memorials or celebrations.

However, even a simple comparison of national actions and

holdings would require far more knowledge than is available to this author. But a quick hint as to their activities will be helpful. The United States, Great Britain and the Commonwealth, the Republic of (South) Korea, the Republic of China, and the Democratic People's Republic of (North) Korea have been the most inclined to maintain records. All have been limited in their celebrations of the war. Interest has expanded somewhat in the past two decades or so. There have been few novels, little poetry, few significant official histories, and little artistic display concerning their participation in the war. Of the Commonwealth nations, Australia has done the most to remember, though they are still publishing more on "who really shot down the Red Baron" than they are on Korea. Few South American nations were involved, and those who were made an economic rather than military contribution.

South Korea, however, has produced hundreds of novels, dozens of well-crafted anthologies, hundreds of films, including the few that are worth seeing, and music both popular and classical. The story of the war is still a story told around the family supper table, and the government's effort to express appreciation to the United Nations, primarily Americans, is lauded.

North Korea, with its limited resources and restrictive government, has managed to record the war in really remarkable movies and films, classical music, artwork, and creatively established museums and memorials. Statues and memorials abound. What is most obvious in the North Korean cultural response is the lack of notice, let alone appreciation, for the involvement of the Chinese volunteers.

The Republic of China itself regards the war as a major event and has called upon its best talents to record it as seen through their eyes. As a whole the work is essentially nationalistic and less dismissive of the United States than one might expect. Recently the Chinese National Archive released (printed) a rather large number of significant documents and suggested that they will continue to do so.

Russia (trustees for the Soviet Union) has generally denied much interest or involvement in the war, but nevertheless is an excellent source of information. It was the opening of their archive that has allowed a whole new phase of histories to be written. As meticulous record keepers, they have preserved a great deal of material that someday may be available.

Preface

*It doesn't do anyone any good to live one life
and hide another.—James Currier*

Whether intentional or not, America's history of misunderstandings, misjudgments, misdirections, denials, and bold-faced lies to Americans and others, has greatly weakened the memory of the Korean War (1950–1953), and led to the loss of many of the significant lessons it might well have taught us. A false sense of the war, evaluated by the American people, has been a default of history and a disservice to those whose lives were greatly affected by this event. It was indeed a conflict that determined the fate of nations as well as defining the generation. But it is considered with little regard for what it meant or what it cost. It has remained a conundrum in American history.

Few Americans recall the police action-turned-war that occurred in Korea. Ironically, the event is best remembered for not being remembered. Even this aspect is a misconception. The truth is that the Korean War has not been forgotten. To forget implies an original knowledge. It suggests that information once held is now gone. And that is not generally the case. There was very little knowledge in the first place. From the beginning, Americans have been uninformed and misinformed about the impact of this war, and thus have allowed an indelible gap to appear in their historical understanding. It has weakened our domestic and international responses in world affairs, as well as failing to provide adequate resources and appreciation for those who fought in Korea.

The case can be well made that the American approach to the Korean War, and the nation's attitude toward its veterans, has been significantly different over the years from its response to the veterans

1

of other wars. Different enough to distinguish a veteran of Korea from those of other wars. Generally silent and unresponsive to much of what has happened, this generation of veterans appears to have created a legacy of quiet acceptance. Their timely and selfless contribution has been primarily unacknowledged. The lessons they might well have taught us have been limited by the fog of public ignorance.

Explanations for much of what has happened can be found by looking deeper into the various social and cultural influences involved, hoping perhaps to consider the context of their attitudes and the rationale for their approaches. Thus one can try to understand what it is that has consistently pushed this Asian war into the dustbin of American history.

It is necessary to begin such an inquiry by acknowledging the effect of the war and that it has been forgotten. To recognize that the causes and curses of what is now called post-traumatic stress syndrome were as prevalent—though neither identified nor acknowledged—among the Korean veterans as it has been since the conflict in Vietnam. In Korea the approach to combat stress was more practical than in World War II, and the suffering individual was treated with the expectation he would quickly be returned to combat. Later studies have shown that the number of men evacuated from the field due to psychiatric reasons was 23 percent during World War II, but during the Korean War it dropped to 6 percent. Surely this suggests either a lower rate of affliction or a much higher degree of tolerance for the condition.[1]

There is no indication of a lower percentage of soldiers suffering, and more current studies have shown that the "go home and work it off" attitude of so many of these damaged men was quietly accepted by a society with little or no interest in prolonging the discussion of the war or its costs. However, while the Vietnam and post–Vietnam veteran appears to have had far more immediate symptoms of trauma, those who served in Korea have illustrated a delay of symptoms, either on the part of the participant or in the public recognition. More and more veterans of Korea are showing symptoms today, fifty to sixty years after the fact.

The Truman doctrine of "guns and butter" allowed the war to be fought on the nation's credit card and removed much of the burden that national conflicts usually impose on its people. Concerned about an already war-weary population, the government never really identified the war for what it was, and deliberately downplayed the event in terms of civilian involvement. The Korean War lacked many of the usual accouterments that one might expect to accompany such a war, things like rationing, shortages, large tax increases, victory gardens, or being emotionalized by Gold Star mothers and star-studded bond rallies. Nothing that was done seemed to have a significant effect on the people's lack of interest in the event. Yet it was an event that should have been of vital national concern.

Not since the War of Jenkins' Ear (1739–1748) have the goals of a war been so unclear to those called upon to fight it. Lacking any dramatic point of entry, like that provided by the Alamo or Pearl Harbor, national involvement in the war required a judgment and justification that was not clearly understood or available. In Korea the supposition of a quick response overrode a considered evaluation, and it was left to later propagandists to help determine the goals of the war itself. Everything from the miscalculation of international communism, to the continued belief that the real war would be launched in Europe, prevented both the diplomatic and military focus the war effort really needed. It was a war fought with the hearts and minds of the home front otherwise occupied. The results were a watered-down American attitude about what the conclusion of a war should entail and the acceptance of an end without victory.

As with any war, the events in Korea began to take on characteristics and myths of their own, and stories were created to accompany unexpected outcomes. Excuses for failure, justifications for unnecessary action, and explanations for events that were basically without explanation, were created to meet the needs. Without the restraints of a critical press, and often lacking good basic information, these myths about the conflict in Korea quickly became excuses rather than explanations. Absorbed by the American people and often uncorrected by the very people whose responsibility it is to provide such protection, and allowed to stand unchecked by time and revision, these misconceptions have been scripted and have acquired the strength of legend. Such invalidities mislead those seeking to understand the significance of the war and its historical mark. Policies and decisions are made on the basis of a past that was never experienced. Whether it is the assumption that we fought to establish a democratic government under

President Rhee, or the muted but overwhelming belief that American soldiers had proven incapable of accomplishing the job they were sent to do, these myths are gradually squeezing out the great truths of the war.

As rotation sent the participants of this war back to the United States, significant numbers of them complained that they did not feel they had returned home. America was different and there was little to no indication that they were being welcomed back or even that they had been missed. The lack of national pride in what had been accomplished had limited any outburst of emotion and curtailed celebration, and so produced few parades. Most newspapers barely mentioned the end of the war, and other than to comment on prisoners, had little continuing coverage. Korea was an entirely different war from the one fought by the "greatest generation" and the clandestine battle in Vietnam, so home-front understanding was limited and the need for it unrecognized. The isolation so often felt on the battlefield had found its way home.

One reason the Korean War has been so poorly imagined by the Americans people is that they know very little about the nature of war itself. Some illustration of the degree to which this is true can be found in the outburst of anger and confusion that followed the disclosure of the massacre at No Gun Ri. The event was a great shock to so many because they didn't know what war was like. They were totally unaware of what they were demanding of their young people and what it was doing to them as well as to the nation. Americans do not talk about war as if it were real, nor do they study war in their schools, nor do they consider the challenge their involvement presents to the moral principles of their religion. They simply do not comprehend the tedium of involvement or the violence of battle. They talk about going to war, about heroics, about victories and accomplishments, but not about war. They can quote leaders, count casualties, applaud victories, but they do not know anything about the impact of organized violence. Little is known about how the very moral fiber of the nations involved has been altered. They make their decisions, they engage their enemies, they extend war as a political ploy, and they do so without understanding war.

The vast silence that represents the events of the Korean War, from the empty shelves in the history section of the bookstore to the lack of musical scores for memorial symphonies, suggests that those to whom we normally look for recording the factual and emotive nature of our national events have not done so. The media has not provided a particularly good service. Nor has the historical discipline managed to focus wide attention on these events in an open and compelling manner. The narrative histories have not offered much intensity in their understanding of the war. As well, the movie industry, a traditional tool for public memory and commemoration, has not only failed to produce the sort of film needed, but has contributed to the many misconceptions by ill-conceived tales poorly told.

The memory of this war, and the voiceless nature of its many veterans, results in a large measure from the haze of suspicion that has hovered over their participation. Right or wrong, the American people were convinced at the end of the war that the average soldier did not perform well and had retreated in the face of danger. Many still believe today that by some mysterious fashion, soldiers who had served in Korea had been subject to and altered by communist brainwashing. The failure of America's finest to defeat a peasant army from a poverty-stricken nation had to be explained somehow, and the soldiers' lack of character became a pivot point. While the suggestions were rampant as the armistice was signed, the scope of the charges lessened somewhat as interest waned. But the assumption did not go away. It has been carried on in part by the veterans themselves, who assumed some of the blame cast upon them and are prone to feel their contribution has been tarnished. The underlying assumption has been an unnecessary burden for the veteran.

The Korean War continues to this day. Along the Demilitarized Zone, the most heavily fortified border on the planet, the nations still face off to exchange daily insults and threats. South Korea, which stands at the threshold of the conflict, has never signed the fragile treaty. Yet whatever peace was achieved has miraculously held, though the conditions that led to war are as strong and present as they ever were. Decisions made at the time of the armistice, from the continued division of the Korean people to the Eisenhower administration's willingness to leave American prisoners of war behind, weakens the agreement. The current inclusion of North Korea as one of the Axis of Evil further stymies discussion and solidifies the path of hostilities.

The Korean War was a watershed in American domestic and

international policies. It changed America and the world in ways that challenge us even today. The full meaning and implications may never be known, perhaps cannot be known, but the war, which was seemingly fought without vision and ended without victory, was nevertheless an essential phase in America's undertaking of itself. For the struggle in Korea not only altered the nature of war itself, it changed the expectations upon which warfare evolved.

This is an effort to identify some of what went wrong with our commemoration and memory as well as our education and insights. The desire is that it will lead to more serious studies. The hope, as well, is that it might initiate an increased appreciation for those who represented our nation in this struggle.

I

Reluctant to Call It War

It ain't what they call you,
it's what you answer to.—*W.C. Fields*

It seems like such a silly thing: whether Korea was a conflict, war, or police action. Who cares? What's the difference? "That which we call a rose/By any other word would smell as sweet."[1] Really? Among the dictates of official language it is hard to create so great a distinction between the categories that it would make a really significant difference. But the simple fact is reflective of a major flaw in our dealing with the events in Korea in the 1950s and is, therefore, an important part of our attempt to understand the role of Korea in the American memory. One easily recalls the early work of Friedrich Nietzsche, the German philosopher who carefully pointed out that the lack of a name leaves an event in *historica absconddita*, that is, what literary critic Pierre Machetrey identified as "structured absence," or the absence of a historical period from the memory of a person or a nation.[2]

It certainly seemed like a war. General Douglas MacArthur, in frustration about the lack of clarity provided in his assignment, proclaimed, "Even if Truman was not waging war against Red China, China was certainly waging war against the United States."[3] Most persons would find little difference between war and conflict, even though the official definition represents a clear distinction. A conflict is a clash between persons, not necessarily armies, that is controlled by those who are participating. That is, those in the action are defined by the conflict. On the other hand, a war is an act of hostilities established by one government against another, with a condition of war proclaimed. Almost all wars contain conflict, but conflicts are not necessarily wars. The confusion associated with the Korean fighting is that it had all the

7

earmarks of a war other than the nation state's willingness to so commit.

The vagueness of status, at least in the mind of the president and some members of Congress, effectively bypassed the constitutional requirement that the Congress be involved in the declaration of war. Given the circumstances, there was some reason to believe that Congress would never have provided the authorization the president wanted, or more important would take so long to act that it would affect the outcome. The executive accomplished his purpose, leaving Congress out of it. A third description, apparently suggested by a reporter but accepted by Truman, was "police action," an identity that weakened the event even more. It was the most distasteful identification for those who participated in the fighting.[4]

For those involved, and for the veterans ever since, these euphemisms suggest the events in Korea were but a heated confrontation worthy of little more than a footnote. For some, it was not even a conflict but a police action. The fighting in Korea was a war in every sense of the word, and describing it otherwise disrespects the efforts of those for whom it was a significant life-changing experience. Police action, the avoidance phrase of the president, reduced the value of participation even further. Truman was a student of history and may have been aware of the previous use of the phrase to identify undeclared action. As of today the United States has fought no declared wars since World War II. The term war has recently been downgraded to mean little more than a fight against something, as in War on Poverty.

Acknowledging that veterans can be somewhat thinned-skinned on the subject, their point is still a valid one. The Korean War needs to be identified for what it was and needs to be registered in America's mem ory for what it is. While narrative histories of the war rarely mention the veterans' disdain for the less historic identification, the letters and memoirs, both published and unpublished, bring it up as a routine concern.[5]

It is never wise to give too much credence to something as seemingly inconsequential as a name, but there is more here than might at first be considered. If nothing else, it made an awful lot of difference to a wide sweep of men who see it as evidence of a nation downgrading their experience, and decreasing the value of their contribution. It is disheartening to realize that your coach considers you the second-string team fighting a lesser conflict, while others are held in reserve for when the real war emerges. Certainly the president would not have had that in mind and few would voice it, but constant downplay of the event, starting with the name, suggested it was not being taken all that seriously. It implied that only a limited commitment should be made in order not to weaken the nation's resources in the face of Soviet hostility that existed elsewhere.

Naming is a matter of recognition, of being brought out of the abstract and identified. The name is the first clue to the significance of the event. If the government was not sure it was a war and the media did not know what to call it, then the society was not all that sure it was a war. The bestowal of a name and identity is a kind of symbolic contract between the society and the person or the event. With a name, the event, like the individual, becomes a part of the history of the society, and takes on a life of its own. "Baby" is a good general acknowledgment of a new life, but when it is named "Dashill" it is separated from the existence of all other living things. The name provides a person or an event both belonging and individualism.

The naming is also significant because it releases a person or an event from the vagueness of the abstract and provides it with an objective reference point to which a memory can be attached. There is no better illustration of this than the power of company logos and brand names, or the Bible account in which God gave man dominion over the beasts of the field by allowing Adam to name them. The name provides the *what* and *how* of that which we recall. In fact, until we address the issues of *what* and *how*, it is almost impossible to remember them.

The name is significant as well in that it establishes the judgment and evaluation of the event. In this case it reflects the moral justification for our action. For there is a difference, albeit primarily in the mind, between being involved in a conflict and in a war. Much of the United States bought into Reinhold Niebuhr's theological justification of its fight against communism, "evil committed in the defense of good is not evil," and many people tended to see Korea more as a response to evil than a war. Once America was involved, and seeking the aid of other nations, the moral issue came up again. This time the government found itself seeking an increase in the involvement of the allies by invoking the moral issue. Even Secretary of State John Foster Dulles, in his search for more allied involvement, reverted to claiming that "neutralism is immoral."

There does not appear to be any way to evaluate the idea that the more names something is called the less each one identifies what it is. At any rate the accumulation of names is a sign of lack of clarity that clouds the understanding of what it is. But in most cases anecdotal evidence suggest that the events in Korea were seen from so many angles that those seeking clarity resorted to all sorts of names. Since Congress finally acted, it is officially known as the Korean War. In all sort of government documents, prior to the distinction and long after, it is referred to as the Korean Conflict, a police action, a limited war, Mr. Truman's War, the Korean Civil War, Unknown War, MacArthur's War, the longest war, the unreal war, or sometimes, particularly by members of Congress, as Truman's Folly.

Many of those in the military referred to it as "the armed aggression" and the "breach of the peace," or sometimes the "prolonged war." In later years it became known as the "forgotten war." During the many debates about the war, members of Congress attached a variety of descriptive names to the events, such as the "dirty war" or "silly war." Max Hastings, the British historian who has provided one of the better narrative histories, describes it as "[u]ndisputedly a frustrating, profoundly unsatisfactory, experience." General Omar Bradley, on several occasions, referred to it "as a great military disaster." S.L.A. Marshal, army historian who always sides with the military, nevertheless described it "as the century's nastiest little war." Ironically the fight in Korea has become best known for not being known.

There is hardly a book or article dealing with the military or political aspect of the war that does not refer to it as the "forgotten war." To the small degree this name contributes to its identify, it places "Korean War" and "forgotten" in the same category. Just what is it that we have forgotten? What was known and understood and then allowed to slip from our memory? For most Americans there is not even an entity well enough defined to have been forgotten. It is a fact that many persons who live in the United States did not know enough about the war to forget it.

The communists have been more direct in the naming of the event, making it very clear and not easily forgotten: China's "War to Resist United States Aggression and Aid Korea," and North Korea's "Fatherland Liberation War," are equally well defined. The communist intent in clearly identifying what happened is particularly interesting when you see the degree to which authors play around with both the terms and the meaning of the event, as in the case of Callum A. Macdonald's book that he called *The War Before Vietnam*.

The word "war" has itself suffered a considerable loss of meaning in the last several decades. In the first place, there are so many conflicts going on that the uniqueness of one nation's passionate aggression against another is lost. For Americans the collage of wars, conflicts, interventions, police actions, peace-keeping missions, and preventive wars, is hard to follow. They sometimes appear as if all were the same war and the distinction between one and another is the location or the enemy's name, or the list of goals to be accomplished. But basically all the same war.

It is true as well that the practice of defining policy and procedure as a "war" has further deflated the term's meaning. The word no longer has to power to identify the degree of hostilities that exists. What is the difference in passion or commitment between a "war on drugs" or a "war on politically incorrect statements"? In previous generations the word "war" had the power to create a reaction, to unite a people, to combine a cause. In fact, one of the few arguments that suggest the Korean events should not be called a war, lies in the fact that it did not engage the passion of the American people as a true war might well have done.

II

Post-Traumatic Perseverance

We are silent about that aspect of the war that causes
us to admit that in part we loved the war, for to do so
would make us mockers to the values that theoretically
we fought to preserve.—*Anonymous*

Contrary to the often-held assumption that Korean War veterans did not suffer from the effects of post-traumatic stress syndrome (PTS disorder), the fact is that they did. They still do. The quiet and individualized manner in which they dealt with the condition has led many to believe that it was less of a problem than that suffered, say, by the Vietnam veterans. The considerable gap that appears to have existed between the time of the trauma and the expression of the symptoms has made any diagnosis difficult. A hazy and poorly understood phenomenon, it has not been properly addressed either as a military or a medical issue, but in both cases, attention to it has increased dramatically, at least in the case of Vietnam and post–Vietnam wars.

The phenomenon was given a medical name in 1980 so the newly affected had some way of identifying it, and thus it took on an identity that it had not had before. Being named, it could now be addressed. During and after the American Civil War, whatever it was that soldiers suffered from was vaguely identified as "Soldier's Heart." In and following World War I, those who suffered this misunderstood condition were said to be suffering "shell shock," as many believed it was caused by the concussion from exploding shells. In the Second World War, it was identified as "battle fatigue" or "traumatic neurosis," and in Korea "the thousand-yard stare." Everyone knew about it, no one paid a lot of attention to it, no one took responsibility for it, and only years later did they start trying to do anything about it.

Once social consideration was aroused, the outspoken Vietnam veterans generated an increasing interest and a search for aid. For a long time, and in a variety of circumstances, the tendency was to consider the shell-shock casualty as merely the manifestation of poor training, bad discipline or even a lack of courage. Since it was caused by the pressure of exploding shells, the cure was to get the disturbed soldier away for a few days. In World War I, the tendency was to treat the condition as a fault of those suffering, and they were often incarcerated. In World War II there was far more awareness and care, but in comparison to other medical issues, it received very little field consideration.

There have been almost no studies that look into the results of battle fatigue among the Korean War veterans. When new interest in such a condition began to emerge in the 1970s, the studies generally just added the name of the Korean War to their reports, assuming the information was the same. What this means is that the psychological problems rampant during the Korean War have faded into the background, and such trauma as might have been experienced has been downplayed. This, of course, does not mean that the Korean veteran did not suffer PTSS in his own and somewhat different way.[1] On the battlefield such anxiety was often treated on line and the soldier was primarily sent back into combat. Many still deal with those concerns. The clues were not much different than those seen today: increased rate of unemployment due to some form of disability, increasing reliance on alcohol or drugs, psychological maladjustment, and a decrease in social and occupational functioning, as well as operating at a much lower level than life expectancies.[2]

World War II veterans came home to a hero's welcome and a booming national economy and were often able to make the peacetime adjustment to civilian life with less dramatic baggage. It was assumed by the society that they would put "all that" behind them and get on with life. And thus, when ramifications appeared, unemployment was on the increase, homelessness abounded, and drug dependence soared, the society provided social norms to be used by which to explain them: lazy, weak, unwilling to cope, and/or a lack of character or courage. But these symptoms were delayed.

A surprising number of cases of PTSS appeared late in life. In the case of the Korean veteran, they were much later, and this in itself led to frequent misdiagnoses of substance dependence or fictional symptoms;

the causes were often blamed on the implications of the veterans' advancing age.[3] Somehow the cause for the delay and the manner in which it happened may have the same root. Today the inclination is to put the development of symptoms into one of three categories: acute, chronic, and delayed onset. It is the last of these that may well explain both the veteran's awareness and the military's lack of immediate interest.

The suggestion seems to be that the Korean veterans who had experienced these feelings were either not as affected by them as veterans in earlier and later wars, or—and this is much more likely—the primary attitude and reaction to the war led the Korean veterans, more than other veterans, to give it much less consideration. A good number of them, having faced their own trials and unique experiences, just came home. Looking about them, they wondered where the glory had gone, made an effort to forget the uneasy dreams and unexplained anxiety, and got busy preparing for life. "Whatever," they said, as they did about so many things, and moved on. You hear very little about this problem from these veterans, not because they did not have such experiences, but they do not talk about it.

Nevertheless, many carried with them the daunting and unexplained anxiety for much of their lives. This feeling has often been identified as sadness. Sadness most certainly appears to be a prevalent common denominator among Korean War veterans. This is a sadness that neither they, nor the few investigators interested, have been able to explain. It emerges out of their sense of loss, of unanticipated isolation, and of forgotten expectations. It is not the sadness of failure, but more the outcome of a subtle grief, which arrives when you are no longer able to deny a major loss. It is found in the awareness that the war, like all wars, took their innocence and left them with little to show for it. It is a sadness that is present without a memory. There is a Korean phrase that says it well: "I am sad because the world is round." It is a longing for home when you are already home.

"We were all a little crazy when we got back," recalled Leon Revere, a Marine speaking with resignation. He then added, "Whatever, I just never let it go." A lot of veterans felt that way but few acknowledged it. Some remembered it with more subtlety, as did this army nurse: "Sometimes I have unaccounted moments when I feel that I have not yet come home." These men and women were not crazy, but many were affected, and it was spread over a much wider variety of veterans than one might have expected. It was not only the result of some horrible confrontation. Military personnel did not have to be in the heart of combat or flying jets over Manchuria in order to have the war leave its mark. Observation as well as participation was a cause, and a sense of responsibility weighed heavy, so peripheral persons such as medics and men of the grave registration units were affected. Some suffered very little, some quite a bit, and a few were badly crippled by their experience. Many of them, no more aware of the source of their uneasiness than were the witnessing public, forged ahead, reporting nothing unusual.

It is particularly noteworthy that the source of much of the recall of previous unpleasant experiences is often simply the effect of the cold. It is a rare Korean veteran who recalls the war and does not remark of his hatred of the cold. The cold, much more than other wars, played a highly significant part, as it resulted from both behavioral and psychological manifestations. The impact of this particular experience has received a great deal of attention from a physical point of view, but the mental impact has not been properly studied when looking at the combat response to the cold.

Acknowledged or not, identified or not, treated or not, Korean veterans shared with other soldiers the shadows of a trauma that changed their lives. We know very little about these cases, the causes and the results, for few have been studied. And most have been conducted with very little empathy. What little research has been done suggests that the degree of stress was affected by rank, with enlisted men suffering the most. Others affected included those with access to strategic information, men whose jobs called on them to make decisions for masses of men, or who carried unreasonable responsibilities. The stress was exaggerated by wounds, which is understandable, and less understandably by the experience of evacuation or retreat.

But, as a general rule, the self-identification of such stress is almost always related to an event in which incredible terror was accompanied by unbelievable acts. The inhumanity was there for all to see and it was difficult indeed not to feel some responsibility. As a group, the veterans suffered far more from problems of mental health[4] than either the society or the government was unwilling to check. In many cases the causes may be fairly easy to identify. But there is as well an underlying haze that reflects the unusual and unexpected anxiety set off by events closer to home and unwittingly imposed by the American people. Our response, seen primarily as apathy, seemed to make the matter worse.

The traumatic experience seems to have led to the fragmentation of our inner selves, often seen as our souls. This experience, when witnessed among American Indians, is called "soul loss," and is considered a disconnect between the body and the soul. Most such cases among primitive people are considered temporary and time is allowed to fix it. It is most easily understood as an adaptive mechanism designed to allow the time needed for healing, and one must wonder if the delay in Korean PTSS is somehow related to this idea. The situation is often identified by feelings of blocked memory, fragmented emotion, limitations on the ability to love or to be loved, and any prolonged social discomfort. Modern cases need more sophisticated treatment, and perhaps some comprehension of the signs of our national apathy that contributed to it.

Another interesting aspect of this feeling of delayed anxiety is found in the fact that many Korean veterans are embarrassed when asked to stand up and be thanked for their service. It seems like an accusation. It started sometime around 1990 and it was not then a common request. By now it has gotten to the point that it means nothing. The public-relations team who included the veterans' recognition in the pre-game warm-up is not interested in the veterans.[5] Veterans acknowledge the good intentions of the local restaurant that offers a free appetizer on Veterans Day and take with good humor the fact that the restaurant failed to list Korea as a war they recognize. It feels like it does when you give a child a gift and the child had to be reminded to thank you. It would have been nice if it had occurred at the time and with some feeling.[6] "We made no ripples," said Frank Kelly, Marine and later minister. "We left and we returned without making a single ripple."

Statistics, like bikinis, often promise more than they expose, but recent considerations have led us to the belief that most of the Korean veterans reacted more strongly, and are more likely to seek some sort of help, the older they get. The reason for this is not easily explained, but records available report that more and more veterans from this war sought help after reaching the retirement age of 65. The obvious downside of this is the more time that passes before the veteran comes to grip with the symptoms and when he seeks help, the more deeply ingrained is the difficulty. Added to the complexity of the problem, many of the symptoms of PTSS are hard to identify as the veteran gets older, because of the cooption of other diseases to explain what is happening. It is easy to explain growing depression with the advance of age, forgetting the trauma of three-quarters of a century earlier.

The more commonly held belief is that as the veterans got older and started to retire, their families primarily raised and their ambitions fulfilled, they had the time to reconsider their lives. Time and emotional freedom were available to consider long-repressed memories and surprising concerns began to rise to the surface. Others suggest the older veteran has been influenced by all the talk generated by Vietnam and Gulf War veterans, and are seeking their share of public awareness. Still others are sure that veterans with weakened physical and mental powers have gradually lost their ability to fight the anxiety. Interestingly, many of these researchers share with the veterans a greater interest in achieving an explanation for what was happening than they are in seeking a cure for it. A surprising number of veterans have voiced the idea that they are primarily interested in identifying the feelings. Few efforts have been made to codify the symptoms, fewer still to identify the home-grown causes for much of their effect.

III

Getting It Straight

The greatest disaster in American history was
when Harry Truman's Kansas City haberdashery
went bankrupt.—*Anonymous*

If we are to understand this war, hundreds of topics need in-depth studies and many assumptions need considerable rethinking, for despite the passage of so many years, there remains far more to be learned about the Korean War than has yet been clarified. From discussions of its origins to the terms of the armistice, many of the major issues have remained clouded, with public opinion and scholarly analyses often at variance. Some of this confusion cannot be helped, as much of the information remains unavailable. Access to Russian archives has eased somewhat, but those of the Republic of China and the Democratic People's Republic of Korea are generally unavailable. The CIA, for reasons not totally clear, is still holding onto some material. It is hoped that in time more open archives and historical cooperation will help clarify a good deal, but as it is now, there are a significant number of questions about which misinformation abounds.

These confusions exist between what appears to be the facts, and what better scholarship has suggested are the facts. That is, what we have been led to believe, and what broader information generally available to us, has altered our understanding of the war and leaves us confused about how it was conducted and how it has affected the nation and the world. Advanced scholarship has forced us to reconsider what at first seemed so evident. The problem continues in that the larger public intelligence, and unfortunately some popular histories, have not kept pace with expanding evidence.

In epistemology[1] there is a phenomenon called "justified true belief" that refers to something that is true for a reason, not just chance or circumstances. This is best illustrated by the person who is in an upstairs room. On the floor beneath him the TV is on. The person hears a siren on a TV show from the floor below and remarks to his companion, "There is a police car outside our door." Suppose at the same time a police car silently comes down the street toward the house in hopes of catching a reported intruder. It parks outside the window. Thus, in fact, the remarks are true. There is a police car outside the window. But not for the reason the person believed. In this case the truth is coincidental, a happenstance, and the fact that he was right has nothing to do with either reason or circumstance. This same idea is well illustrated in the statement that the North Koreans started the war, which may well be true, for it appears they first crossed the 38th parallel. But the true "cause of the war" may result from different reasons—reasons that have very little to do with the first aggressive act.

The following considers a few examples of the disparity between public knowledge and justified true beliefs. Some are fairly simple to address, others more complex.

North Korea Started the War

Advanced scholarship by such esteemed historians as Kathryn Weathersby and Alan Millett have exposed the complexities of domestic and international pressures at work behind the outbreak of violence in Korea. The fact of the North Korean invasion and the assumption of a policy of containment may suggest a cut-and-dried answer as to causes. The North Korean government under the leadership of Kim Il Sung started the war.

But the answer may be far more complex than this fact would suggest. Many factors, from the decision to liberate South Korea, to the culmination of interlocking anticommunist alliances, were present at the beginning. Before 1970 or so, most academic literature tended to downplay any other origin than that of the communist invasion, but after that time, more investigations led to the understanding that it was a more complex event than simply crossing a parallel.

The victory of the Communist Party in China in 1948, the Soviet explosion of a nuclear weapon, and the powerful, often extreme, influence of Senator McCarthy and others obsessed with domestic communism, would have made it difficult for Truman to do nothing in response to this intrusion of North Korean forces. The other side of this is suggested by Dr. Cummings, who hints that the beginning of the war might well be traced back to the collapse of Japan in 1945 and that the action five years later was already destined by events.

So, while the evidence shows a simple invasion at the crack of dawn, the affirmation that the communists started the war is not sufficient to address the complexities of the various nations' involvement. While the opposing argument, "the United States started the war in Korea," could not be considered to be true in light of the evident invasion, it is nevertheless a somewhat justified truth considering the American responsibility for the events that led to an armed confrontation. Certainly there was talk in the South about an invasion of the North. President Rhee made no bones about the fact that he favored such a move as the means of reunification. The Koreas, after their long struggle against the Japanese, tended to victimize themselves as a part of their own self-perception as the most harassed and occupied people on earth. They were anxious to settle both the question of unification and independence.

On several occasions, especially with his longtime friend and fellow Princeton student John Foster Dulles, Dr. Rhee argued for a preemptive attack. In this case, the Korean Military Advisory Group[2] as well as his own generals, advised against it. Realistically, South Korea had a poorly trained and badly equipped army that was plagued by corruption and defection and was in no position to attack. Aid to Korea had been erratic and unpredictable prior to the outbreak of the war,[3] and Rhee was short of supplies. Despite concentrated efforts, Rhee could not convince the State Department to support his request for heavy equipment. The State Department was afraid to arm Rhee any further for fear he might well launch a march to the North. On the other side of the coin, the People's Republic of China had transferred some 3,000 members of the People's Liberation Army to the North Korean Army.[4]

Initial assumptions tend to suggest that Joseph Stalin was behind the war. He apparently believed that the United States would not intervene in a conflict since he saw no evidence of United States' maintaining any political or military interest in Korea. The U.S. interests apparently were more directed toward the defense of Japan and did not include any penetration into Korea. In addition, the conventional wisdom in Washington was that North Korea could not have mounted an attack on the south without direct aid from Moscow. But standing on more middle ground, revisionist Bruce Cumings has assumed that while Kim Il Sung probably consulted with Stalin, it was Kim who planned and executed the war. There is the hint in Cumings's commentary that the attack may have been in retaliation to provocations set off by the South. Or that the attack was orchestrated by Chinese nationalists (Taiwan) and United States agents who were eager to reassert the American presence in Asia. This is not too far-fetched but certainly increases the difficulty in assessing blame.[5] In general Cumings's work is an assault on America's moral behavior during the war, and the failure of American policy is misremembered when it is remembered at all. Americans must somehow get past the idea that the war in Korea was a discrete, encapsulated story started by communist aggression and the United States decision to intervene. What resulted was "an appallingly dirty war."[6]

William Stueck, in his highly insightful work *Korean War in World History*, however, provides the strongest evidence that the origins of the war can be located in Stalin's belief that such a conflict might well be in the best interests of the Soviet Union. Stalin's expression to Mao Zedong that he was "willing to help him in this matter" is certainly evidence of interest and the possibility of involvement. However, to respond to an attack is one thing; to react to national and international pressures is another. Korean historian Park Ming Li, in considering the role of the two men, has concluded that Kim Il Sung might well have been the initiator of the war and Joseph Stalin the facilitator.[7]

Kathryn Weathersby, with the advantage of having worked in the Soviet archive, shows that North Korea's initial attack on the South was not in response to South Korean raids against the North. Rather, because of the need for support if a war was to be undertaken, Joseph Stalin is the only one who could supply that support and thus would have made the "essential decision."[8]

Chen Jian, Hu Shin Professor of Chinese history at Cornell University, suggests that as far as China was concerned the decision to enter the war not just to protect her frontier but because it would be good for the state to win a fight against the United States. Such a victory would ease the controversy between the Chinese military and society, and promote a revision of China as the dominant power in Asia.[9] In understanding the situation it is important to remember that the Communist Chinese had won a civil war, but the nation was nevertheless economically shaky and the government not entirely consolidated. The ongoing struggle with the nationalists was taking a toll. So, while Mao had a volunteer army of about 5 million, he lacked naval and air weapons, and most of the soldiers were regulars. Allan Whiting said that the decision to fight was finally made by what might have been little other than an unambiguously compelling threat to their security.[10] It was also important to indicate to the world that the Chinese were communists and not unreliable within the socialist camp.[11]

Obviously the question is not settled and will not be until there is more availability of documents from the nations involved. The easy assumption that the war started with a sudden onset, like the attack on Pearl Harbor, is misleading at best. The long political manifestations, the assumption of Moscow's involvement, and belief in the communists' innovation has the tendency to push all other understanding aside. Intelligence since then, as well as new documentation now, suggest there is far more to this than what has yet been discovered.

All "Commies" Are Alike

In the Western world the term communism, like that of socialism, has been bandied about as the ultimate evil since the 1920s. Given a short reprieve during World War II when we found ourselves linked with the Soviet Union against Germany, it nevertheless remained a potential enemy. Any common knowledge of these ideologies had pretty much been reduced to the belief that socialism is a government that owns all things and communism is a system in which a single party runs all aspects of the government. There is some truth in both views but not a lot. There is little popular understanding that communism, like our more favored democracies, might well have divisions of complexity. This means we tend to treat all communist states alike when in fact they are not all alike. A degree to which this monolithic view proved wrong is illustrated in the breakup of the Soviet Union in December of 1999.

As far as our reaction in Korea is concerned, the problem was not in a definition but in the mistaken belief that all communists have the same agenda, that somehow China, North Korea, North Vietnam and Russia, as well as all the related states, were puppets and not independent nations. Thus, if one understands the wishes of one people or the goals of one government, then you supposedly knew the thinking of all. The accompanying assumption was that they all had the same expectations and motivations, and the same methods for achieving what they wanted. Their individual actions and behavior were to be seen in the policies of Moscow, the mother. This was a mistake.

This monolithic view led to considerable misunderstanding about the national and international implications and fed into the belief that a worldwide communist conspiracy was a reality. As well, the belief that communist sympathizers saturated America, lying in wait for the moment to take over, led many to believe in a single "conspiracy" that was willing to use military force to ensure its expansion.

While the communism of the Soviet Union, the People's Republic of China and the Democratic People's Republic of Korea were all rooted in the basic themes of Karl Marx, none of them could be considered an adequate representation of the founder. Some vastly oversimplified comparison might suggest enough differences to argue that the Western approach would have been more effective if based on the different national attitudes of the nations involved, rather than on their similarity. Hailed as a battle cry for the far right, "a commie is a commie no matter where they be," is simply not true.

In the late 1940s and early '50s the Soviet Union dominated this ideological bloc, but the rebellion in China began to illustrate some basic underlying differences. The same was true of the increasing nationalism of North Korea. The Workers' Party joined with the New People Party to form the Workers' Party of Korea. In China, Mao's view was far more nationalistic and based on a belief, not in the workers' revolution that Marx called for, but in an independent agrarian revolution. Spurred on by the political weakness of the national bourgeoisie, the movement grew from the peasant farmers against feudalism and bureaucracy.

At the time of the war, the government in Korea was an ill-fitting collection of four communist factions. Of these, the Soviet faction was composed of those who saw their future tied to Moscow and the more traditional beliefs of Marx and Lenin. A second was the Domestic faction that consisted mostly of industrial workers with primary ties to their Korean heritage. The third, often called the Guerrilla faction, was led by Kim Il Sung and sprung out of the early occupation by the Japanese. The last of these was the Yandi Party, was primarily identified by its ties to China. The government, while considered strong, was not focused, and most certainly was not yet clear in its national concerns. Factions within the group would continue to foster disagreement and sometimes compromise.

Adapted from but not committed to the concepts put forth by Lenin, the Chinese government at this time was run and staffed by members of the party. The party was the government, and it functioned as executed by members of the party in assigned positions. In comparison, the Soviet Union at this time was primarily controlled by the communist party, but the party did not officiate. What the United States needed to keep in mind is that while the Soviet legislature is primarily a puppet, the Chinese legislature represents different factions and thus is the source of discussion and disagreement. Mao did not have the more isolated authority that Stalin enjoyed.

Land distribution within the soviet system was based on government ownership and was organized collectively as Stalin moved to replace the old peasant farmer with "collective farms" on which the peasants worked for the greater good of the party. The Chinese, on the other hand, had a system based on goals established for farm production, in which the government took what was established as the national goal, and for the public interest, and the farmer could keep the rest. In Russia the push was for the urbanization of the people as they gathered workers for the industrial growth of the nation.

Social evolution is another key by which the distinctions of the three communist nations are identified. The Chinese thought progress was economically determined, while in Russia economic evolution was politically driven, with various leadership positions guiding and directing the growth. The cultural flow of the nation's emergence was also different, for in the Russian system the elite class, such as it was, flourished as thinkers, teachers, artists, as well as scientists and social scientists, all held advanced positions and were encouraged, though generally state controlled, in their work. The Chinese, in a series of upheavals, have focused on the simple concerns of the peasant and discouraged the elite, if not actually dislodging them from their work.

In winning the civil war, Mao had necessarily aligned himself with a variety of factions, some of which were primarily anti-communistic, and which had to be dealt with as he consolidated his government. He did this by what is often identified as gradualism, the slow but sure progress toward his defined goal. North Korea had no such limitations, and backed by Russia in the early years, could make more radical and lasting changes with minimal attempt to pacify the dissenters.

For Americans, their involvement in the war was a part of the movement to stop the spread of communism. The ideology, like a disease, was spreading across Europe and engulfing one people after another. It had to be stopped or at least contained. The problems in Korea were partially lost in the underlying feelings that the Soviet Union had to be stopped and that sooner or later it would be necessary to draw a line in the sand. "Are you now, or have you ever been a member of the Communist Party?" was our great concern, and it mattered little what color, or shape, or degree of communist you might be.

Looking at the events *ex post facto* it is much easier to see the nations involved did not all look, or think, or act alike. But when dealing with these events as historical encounters there is still that tendency to assume the monolithic nature of our enemies. It was not true then, and it is not true now.

MacArthur Crossed the 38th on His Own Initiative

As the war expanded, the common myth emerged that China had entered the war primarily as a military support for the people of North Korea, and secondarily to prevent American troops from advancing toward the Yalu River. The Chinese reacted in this fashion, the story goes, because General Douglas MacArthur took it upon himself to take the Eighth Army across the 38th parallel and into North Korean territory. Every evidence is that this was not the case. In the first place, MacArthur did not make the decision, but rather acted on the authority of the Truman Administration and in response to a resolution passed by the United Nations. But there is also a lot of evidence that the general's attitude and behavior may well have been a part of the Chinese decision. Once again the "justified true belief" is hampered by the universal failure to note the difference between an action and a cause.

The facts may well be that the Chinese decision to enter the war was based on the United States' troops crossing over into the north. That is not totally clear. But it most certainly was not the cause. It was, so to speak, a matter of crossing a line in the sand that had been set up after considerable discussion and debate. The decision was far more diversified and was made with somewhat more justifications than the rather arbitrary myth suggests.

First of all, despite the general belief to the contrary, General Douglas MacArthur did not cross over the 38th parallel into North Korea while acting on his own. The decision, often reflected upon as an immediate and instinctive one, was the result of a proposal considered by the Joint Chiefs of Staff. Like all such decisions, it was made by commander in chief, and resulted from a resolution, albeit of questionable legality, by the members of the United Nations.

It appears that MacArthur, President Truman, and the newly formed CIA did not believe the Chinese would react to such a move and that the war needed to be concluded with the destruction of the North Korean army. The discussion conducted among members of the Truman administration and the Joint Chiefs of Staff tended to believe MacArthur's assessment of the situation, and that such an action would not initiate war with the Soviet Union.

Thus on 9 September 1950 the decision was made and orders drafted for MacArthur: "Your military objective is to destroy the North Korean armed forces." The commander was authorized to cross over the 38th parallel and take the war to the North in order to accomplish this mission.[12] A United Nations resolution shortly followed. Troops of the Republic of South Korea had already crossed the line and were moving north with little opposition.

The decision is hard to justify. Truman's advisors may well have given him poor advice. More than one historian has suggested that the opinion resulted from their own lack of decisiveness and a significant fear of insulting MacArthur. Looking back, it seems to have been the last chance to avoid this march to disaster. Joseph Goulden is quick to place the blame, suggesting that the Pentagon was obsessed with timidity, the Joint Chiefs of Staff cowering "before MacArthur like a schoolboy in front of the town bully."[13]

It is apparent that Chairman Mao was inclined to make such a decision, and pushed for it, being concerned not only with China's physical security, but perhaps as importantly, to seek a significant victory over the American forces. The Chinese were apparently not all that concerned if South Korean soldiers entered the North, but the presence of Americans as far north as the Yalu River was simply unacceptable. They would, Mao's government decided, "resist U.S. aggression and aid Korea."

But, as we will discuss later, there was more to it than this. Underlying this approach is the CCP leadership's understanding of the need to consolidate their victory over the Nationalist Chinese. In particular this reflected Mao's desire to protect his new nation from any threat to their sovereignty, but also to energize the Communist Party's control of the state. Having won his civil war and gained domestic control over the nation, it was now necessary for him to regain international recognition and respect. Put more dramatically, Mao sought to strengthen his "control, unify his nation, and seek some international recognition, but he did not seem interested in expanding the nation's military control over his neighbors, including Korea."[14]

Acheson Authorized War

The facts are pretty well known and generally uncontested; it is just that their meaning and importance have been poorly understood. As in earlier cases, the attempt to evaluate the known facts are hampered by a vast array of assumptions. The story, recorded in far too many places, is that Secretary of State Dean Acheson delivered an address to the members of the National Press Club on 12 January 1950. In these much-heralded remarks, the Secretary reported on American interests throughout the world. He did so in such a way as to suggest that the Korean peninsula was not included in America's sphere of interest. As it was, Acheson spoke rather openly to America concerning the difficulties that faced the nation, about global commitments and the need to preserve American influence, but given the size of the problem, to do so in a responsible manner. Korea was just not that important. The occupational troops located there after the war had been withdrawn. The Korean Military Advisory Group (KMAG) had been established to help the South develop its military forces. Washington considered the greatest danger in Korea to be President Rhee's "inability to meet the demand of his people for more democracy, or make a foolish attempt to launch an invasion."[15]

Many have been quick to report that Joseph Stalin, hearing that America was not interested in Korea, then initiated or at least permitted a war in Korea. What became known as Acheson's "open invitation" to Moscow was widely distributed and found its way into a good many histories. James Stokesbury's early narrative history reports the incident in such a way that it does not discredit the charge against the Secretary of State. A later and much more widely used reference work, *Fire and Ice* by Michael J. Valhalla, presents it without comment.[16] Even Dwight D. Eisenhower, while campaigning for the presidency in 1952, charged Dean Acheson's speech with giving the green light to a North Korean invasion because it convinced the communists that America would not defend the south.

Granted, Acheson—who had a well-publicized dislike for the United Nations and felt the nation's interests best lay in Europe and not Asia—made such a statement. But it was far from covering new ground and certainly disclosed no secrets. In fact it correctly reflected the military view that Korea was of no military significance.

But the story is here to stay. As late as 2010 and several years after the release of the Soviet archive, an address reported by National Public Radio explained that a key moment in the chronology of the Soviet decision to be involved in the Korean War came when Acheson left Korea out of his description of America's sphere of influence as he saw it in January 1950.[17]

Under such a point of view, the question about Stalin's willingness to support a war becomes more clouded. The misinterpretation of the comments have stained Acheson's long public service, and provided the predisposition to blame him and MacArthur for the expanded war, and to provide a simple excuse, however wrong, for the communist aggression. Certainly Acheson, as much as anyone in Truman's inner circle, favored a hard attitude toward Korea and later Vietnam, but he did not release the dogs of war.

There Was a Conspiracy

For those who seek one, there is always a conspiracy to be found. Americans in particular seem to love them. This is no less true for

Korea than any other event. Most are extreme and of little value other than keeping the story alive. Some are the products of strange-minded persons who find information where none may exist, or frightened people looking for answers to questions not well asked. Most, however, are concocted by serious inquirers who, right or wrong, believe they have the evidence of a conspiracy. In this case it is an effort to lead the United States to war with Korea.

These hidden agendas are often blamed on established groups who, in one way or another, have been seen in such roles previously. They include international bankers, New World advocates, the military-industrial complex, the communists, or perhaps the Nationalist Chinese. A serious look at the idea of conspiracy is hampered by any real clear view of what a conspiracy is, but assuming it means plans or actions by clandestine units to achieve a particular agenda, then there is reason to give consideration to the idea. After all, what is government other than a conspiracy of one form or another?

Two such men—I.F. Stone, an early journalist and critic, in his early book *The Hidden History of the Korean War 1950–1951: A Nonconformist History of Our Times*, and Dr. Bruce Cumings, a highly recognized historian and author of revisionist history[18]—are on the serious side of this idea. A much lesser known voice, but a loud one for a time, was Congressman John E. Rankin (D–Mississippi), an initial member of the House Un-American Activities Committee, who viewed the Korean War as an extension of the European war orchestrated by the Soviet Union, the Jews, the United Nations, and domestic communists.

Stone was an early revisionist who did not buy into the simple fact of a North Korean invasion, and saw a much wider case for presenting South Korea as the aggressor. The unprovoked war that followed was part of the well-laid plans designed to involve the West in a confrontation with the communists. It was, he felt, in the larger sense an obvious part of America's well-documented aversion to organized labor both in America and overseas.

Writing while the war was still in process, Stone believed that President Truman had been hoodwinked into taking such decisive action by the hawks, led in part by such powerful men as Douglas Mac-Arthur, John Foster Dulles, Dean Acheson, and Syngman Rhee. Later, as a part of this same plan, he believed that both the Republic of Korea and the United States were dragging out the peace talks in order to keep the threat of communism on the front burner. America needed an enemy in order to maintain a united front, and many were working behind the scenes to provide one.

He did not have a lot of followers, but is still respected today for his insights at the time. Historian Claude Bordet commented, "If Stone's thesis corresponds to reality, we are in the presence of the greatest swindle in the whole of military history … not a question of a harmless fraud but of a terrible maneuvered deception is consciously utilized to block peace at a time when it was possible."[19] The historian did not buy Stone's thesis that America was in desperate need of an outside enemy and that North Korea and the war were straight from "central casting."[20]

Bruce Cumings's more recent scholarship sees much of what happened as a part of President Rhee's plan to dominate the nation under his own ruling party. He substantiates his view by quoting General MacArthur "that in fact the war had been initiated by attacks from South Korea during 1948–1950." But his comments go far beyond this. He was aware that commanders of various armies had been forced to select different sides as the nation broke up and would see a clash at the borders as an effective way to carve out their own positions. Regardless of the more immediate details, Cumings appears to believe that the South Korean provocation was the most credible of the possible explanations.[21]

Granted there were a lot of strange things happening in history at this time and that the identification of a conspiracy was one way to handle them. Take, for example, the Merchants of Death of World War I, or the popular belief that President Roosevelt had advance warning of the attack on Pearl Harbor, or such questionable situations as the delegate from the Soviet Union who just happened to be boycotting the United Nations at the very moment the USSR could have vetoed UN involvement in Korea. How, if there was no "other" or "hidden" agenda, do you explain why the United States and the Soviet Union would both remain totally silent about the fact their warriors were clashing in open warfare in the skies over Korea?

Not to be left out, even the Illuminati has raised its ugly head as some found it involved in the initiation and execution of the Korean War. What they wanted was to validate the United Nations as a force for peace and give the Jewish community further control over world affairs. These and many others appear as explanations or, in some cases, accusations. But they are not worth much time.[22] What is evident, however, is that the conspiracy theorist and the misinformed share one thing in common: a willingness to believe without adequate evidence.

And there is always the question of why. Who would, and for what reasons, be interested in such an elaborate plan? Maybe the missionaries in Korea who took such an aggressive role. What would be gained? And besides, most people are just not smart or well organized enough to plan and carry out such a effort. Or, realistically, are unable to keep their mouths shut about such an adventure. Certainly far less dramatic than conspiracy, there have been several persons who saw the war as a plot or plan directed and carried out by a variety of troublemakers with an international agenda; the evidence is as yet uncollected.

Conspiracy is far too simple an answer. But the fact some hold onto it further identifies the impact of the lack of essential information, and the degree of serious scholarship that is still required.

Rhee Was a Democratic Giant

One needs to go no further in search of an established myth that misinforms than to accept the well-programmed nonsense that America's intervention in the fighting in Korea was primarily an act of idealistic altruism.[23] There is little to support the idea that the war was fought for the love of humanity or in the hope of supporting a democratic government. It makes great copy but is short on facts.

The history of America's earlier relations with Korea reads like a cookbook for disaster. It is hard to believe that the United States actually set out to explain this war as the result of our natural love for a people in a land we did not understand, to fight for the preservation of a way of life with which we did not agree. The politicians would remark that the veteran had been called "to defend a country you never knew and a people you never met."[24] That much is true, but unfortunately, every effort to provide the war with some hint of moral significance, thus an effort to attach some degree of support for freedom, is ill conceived.

The United States was far from having arrived at any easy relationship with the leftover baggage of the "yellow peril." Our record of

31

dealing with the Korean people was shaky at best, and was compromised by a series of actions that were of questionable virtue. There is little to suggest that Korea was essential to American interests or that there was any imperial value to our involvement. There certainly was no tradition of democratic relationships. Any attempts to relate what happened there to some moralistic cause, or even a pragmatic necessity, obscures the more complex and realistic understandings of what was happening.

The myth reads: "The exiled leader Syngman Rhee (1875–1965) was exalted as a friend of the United States and the only one who could save the Korean people who loved him. As a firm defender of freedom and democracy, he required our support." His dedication to the nation during years of exile had provided him a powerful base of supporters.

The fact is that Rhee was no friend of the United States and he was not necessarily the selection of the Korean people. Rather he maintained control through harsh political infighting. The view of Rhee as a democrat is a drastic distortion of what happened and ignores the long and desperate struggle to keep Rhee in check.

He was, at best, a convenient straw man suggested by the Nationalist Chinese leader General Chiang Kai-shek, and then by General Douglas MacArthur. He was not democratic, but was rather a despot who used extreme methods to keep control. The government he put together was at best a sham democracy, and Rhee was its tyrannical leader. The American support for this man—a strange, egomaniacal, paranoid, and ruthless character—was, when seen in its best light, a tautological justification based on the fact Rhee was highly anti-communistic. The man, and the behavior of his government, was so unreliable and unpredictable that the American military were justifiably afraid of him. Rhee was a vehemently anti–Japanese, anti-communist, nationalistic leader who wanted to unify Korea through armed intervention in the North. A graduate of Princeton University, he was nevertheless not interested in the American idea of democracy and believed in violence and manipulation to enforce his policies.

Eighth Army Command maintained an operational plan—Operation Everready—that was kept in place during the entire war to orchestrate a coup if necessary to expel Rhee and set up a military government to control Korea.[25] It is not all that unusual for military and civilian leaders to find themselves involved in the political paradox of fighting to defend a nation or a leader whose very ideals and expectations are in opposition to our own rhetoric about democracy and freedom. This was the case in Korea. Over time we have fairly easily ignored the reality of places like Seoul, Saigon, Baghdad and Kabul. In supporting Rhee, we supported a totalitarian government.

Korea Was a Ploy

A great deal of consideration has been given to the environment that led to the North Korean attack on South Korea. While most of them are focused on events in Asia and the aggressive tone of the Cold War, some have felt that understanding it requires us to realize that it was most likely intended as a ploy to distract the West from events in Europe. While it is understandable that people might look to the larger picture for answers, the practice of doing so with such a broad scope has had the potential of skewing more realistic and justifiable causes.

Such a view does present some interesting corollaries. Not the lease of these is the degree to which Truman was aware that his administration's involvement in Asia had the potential of undermining the endorsement the United States had made to its strategic allies in Europe. At the same time it has the tendency to weaken our understanding of the Soviets' interest in Asia, and how a war in Korea might well play into that scenario. Once again, thinking in this fashion was inclined to confuse the administration's view of the Soviet bloc, or the degree to which the satellite states were either directed or motivated by Moscow. The United States had other military concerns, of course. Basic to these was unrest about what the Soviet intentions were. The Department of Defense needed as many resources available in their command as well. In 1948, probably as a result of the Berlin blockade, the United States transferred nearly half the Far East Air Force (B-29) against the strong objections of General MacArthur. The war was being fought in Korea, but the fear of war, and the expectations of hostilities, remained in Europe.

The irony of this assumption had the far more practical implication of undermining the war in Korea. It meant that Truman, with one eye on troop movements in Europe, was sending men and materials, money and effort to NATO that might otherwise have been available for the more pressing conflict. Herein lies some of the answer to the question why United Nations troops were so often short of supplies, even ammunition. The answer was, at least in part, that men coming out of the replacement camps, weapons being developed and updated, and funds being expended were going to Europe. This fact was not well explained to, or understood by, either the home front or the GI in Korea who was still wearing his summer uniform in December. The military was simply not in the position to meet all the needs imposed by our worldwide involvements. Early histories are more inclined to address the idea of a ploy but do not explain it well. For example, James L. Stokesbury, I.F. Stone, and T.R. Fehrenbach in *This Kind of War: The Classic Korean War History.*[26] Many of the later histories, particularly the popular works that started coming out in the 1980s, often fail to mention the idea of a ploy at all.

It is hard to identify just how widely the ploy was accepted by the president's staff or to create some numerical accounting of the conflicting support of Korea and NATO. The war in Korea was loud and easily focused people on its immediate threat, but every evidence today suggests that Stalin was no more interested in war with the United States than Truman wanted a fight with the Russians. The Chinese leader Mao was so aware of its domestic implications that he refused to even call it a war. Nevertheless the idea of a ploy played a role that is still being determined.

MacArthur Was Fired for Insubordination

During his life, General of the Army Douglas MacArthur was one of those persons whom people tended to love or to hate. The battle lines on that issue have never been clearly drawn, as many veterans continue to identify him as "Bug Out Doug," based on his untimely withdrawal from Bataan in World War II. Still others consider him as the source of victory in Japan. Most scholars writing about him admit that he was a complex personality who will probably never be understood. He was, and has been, a mystery clouded in an enigma.

There is little doubt that he had vast military and administrative abilities, and despite his arrogance, he was highly successful during World War II. He had created for himself a national popularity, and when he was fired in April 1950, there was a great uproar among the American people. Spurred on by uninformed commentaries and generally aware of the rebellious nature of the general's personality, many accepted the idea that President Truman fired him for insubordination. Certainly there was no lack of evidence that he had allowed himself and his staff to act in a manner contrary to specific orders from the president, and was thus guilty of the charges.

Much of the argument for insubordination emerged as anecdotal stories of his challenging authority and getting away with it. More contemporary beliefs are represented in the views of Secretary of State Dean Acheson, who wrote in his incredible autobiography *Present at the Creation*, "It seems impossible to overestimate the damage that General MacArthur's willful insubordination and incredible bad judgment did to the United States." He goes on to cite examples, many of which continue to appear in the myth of the firing. MacArthur failed to carry out the orders, he reported, "to fight a limited war within the confines of Korea itself, to keep his American troops behind a fixed line and away from the Chinese border, to keep his bombers from Chinese and Soviet territory, and to refrain from denouncing his orders and criticizing the President in messages to the press and Congress."[27]

But this is far too simple an answer and was clouded by other charges. In informing the nation of his action in the dismissal of the general, Truman hinted at a challenge to the civilian control of the military. There is much evidence that the former was true and very little evidence of the latter case being true, but both myths stuck. The latter idea, considered in detail by Amy Patterson, Wynell Schamel and Lee Ann Potter in "The Firing of General Douglas MacArthur during the Korean War," makes the point that such a challenge had been consistent and accumulative.[28]

This argument was the easiest to sell. Several biographies appeared that suggested the insubordinate actions of a general in his relations to the president of the United States. And in the acceptance of the view, these works have failed to see the larger, more significant situation. Hovering in the background is the much less dramatic justification. The two men held opposing positions on Asian policy, and only the president could win such an argument.

One must suspect from reading Truman's memos that he did not like the general. Truman once privately referred to the general as a coward for leaving Corregidor.[29] In an interesting but poorly distributed talk given to the Veterans of Foreign Wars, D.C. Ginoreco of the Command and Staff College suggests some bad blood was established when the two of them met on the battlefield of Meuse Argonne. While the president never referred to this, he did interfere in the writing of the official history of World War I in order to tone down some of the accomplishments listed for the Marines at that battle.[30]

But it was not insubordination that worried the president and his staff, nor was it a challenge to constitutional authority. It had to do with the question of who established national policy. Asian policy, if it was really ever clear enough to be so identified, was established after the war had begun and was reflective of lessons learned or policies failed, and in terms of the broader projections for the area. There is no doubt that MacArthur wanted to move against China, and that he believed he was in a position of strength to do so. Reflecting a view not that much different from General Patton's argument against communism at the end of World War II, he believed it was necessary to intensify the war to whatever degree would be required for victory.

In such an action they could settle the question of American influence in Asia once and for all. The general made no bones about the fact that he was not in sympathy with the increasingly limited nature of the American response and made no effort to hide his disagreement when he talked with other world leaders. While he gathered some support for his idea, what many saw as the practicality of the situation required a different approach.[31]

Despite the fact that the Joint Committee on the Armed Services and Foreign Affairs report on the investigation suggested that "the Joint Chiefs had no disagreement with MacArthur on Korean policy," their part in the decision to dismiss him was unanimous. The extent of his view led General Bradley, Chairman of the Joint Chiefs of Staff, to provide the administration's rather definitive position when he remarked that a war with China "would be the wrong war at the wrong time against the wrong enemy."[32] When considering MacArthur's behavior, and his later plan for winning a war in China, General Eisenhower commented in his diary (1954), "I just cannot understand how such a damn fool could have gotten to be a general."[33] In his early writings, historian James Stokesbury reaffirmed the view that the general was relieved for his lack of support for the Truman policies, but he also admitted openly that the general was insubordinate.[34] It was sometimes hard to tell the difference.

For both political and face-saving reasons, the quick acceptance of the insubordination theory and its long-lasting memory may have been very successful. Most persons failed to see the policy argument in its largest context and were ill-equipped to judge how MacArthur's actions were destructive to America's Asian alignment. Voicing a concern about the attitude of the American people, General Bradley commented to the Joint Chiefs of Staff, "If General MacArthur was not relieved, a large segment of our people would charge that the civil authorities no longer control the military."[35]

Of course, the acceptance of the easy answer draws attention away from the debate over the policy itself. It makes it simpler to divert the discussion away from the deeper national issues and allows it to appear as a dispute of personalities. The continued belief that the general's demise reflects concern over the "question of civilian control" belies the complexes of concerns that faced the Truman administration at the time.

Nevertheless, in the context of the man in question, it was almost a necessity for him to leave his years of public service in the midst of such a debate. For a man who had made a reputation as a maverick, the insubordinate general was following his own star. Such a man, many less informed chroniclers assumed, would not have been nearly as well remembered if his dismissal was simply for a disagreement in policy.[36]

As the war progressed, the general proceeded to gradually fade away.

The CIA Knew All Along

Back when CIA meant Commissioner of Indian Affairs, most military intelligence was conducted by the Army in the field and was little more than reconnaissance. But the success of the various intelligence services during World War I, especially within the British government, and then again in the Second World War, suggested the need for a unified intelligence effort. The widely scattered programs and the general lack of cooperation between them was standing in the way of the accomplishment of their goals. Thus, eventually the Central Intelligence Agency (1946) was established and the myth began. Designed to be secretive and authorized by the president for questionable activity, it became the byword for describing vague clandestine governmental activities. Born with few friends and a good many enemies, the agency's initial efforts were mainly hampered by low budgets and limited staff.

Two intelligence groups were assigned responsibility for keeping the Far East Command aware of what was going on with the enemy. The CIA was fairly new and primarily located outside the area, and the G-2 Section of MacArthur's Far East Command was located in Tokyo. From the beginning, in good measure because of the secret service (OSS) background of many of its operatives, the agency tended to be more interested in covert actions than the collection of intelligence as we think of it today. Truman did not want another Pearl Harbor, and he expected the CIA to provide full warning. As it turned out, they did not.

Many of the "I was there" memoirs that came out after the war, as well as novels and movies based on them, have perpetuated the myth that the CIA provided intelligence concerning the intentions of the Chinese and North Korean government and that the American military acted upon such information. Such a telling, while good reading, ignores what must have been two or three of the most inexcusable intelligence failures in world history. And despite the courageous actions of some men and women during the Korean War—primarily partisans—the ability of the CIA to predict military action or provide information about communist intentions was not only useless, it was incredibly dangerous.

While there is no shortage of evidence that the political and military leaders took limited advantage of what little intelligence was being provided, it is also true that the data available was so often late or irrelevant that the agency was unable to generate the reputation needed for the worldwide intelligence service it was intended to be. Between poor collection, inadequate comprehension, improperly trained and misguided analysis, the CIA's role in the intelligence community during the Korean War was less than adequate.

The problems were not all internal. Generally the opposition from other agencies made it difficult for the CIA to establish itself. In Asia its potential as a helpful tool was considerably limited by the fact that General MacArthur disliked and distrusted the agency and did all he could to keep them out of Japan and Korea. He even refused them an office until ordered to do so. As it was, the agency's preparation for involvement was totally inadequate and grossly misunderstood. There were, for example, no Korean speakers on the staff.

It was only when the CIA took it upon itself to create a reputation that the mood began to change. Over the next few years the agency reversed the situation and came to hold a reputation for efficiency, one they had not earned and did not deserve. In the popular mind, the CIA in Asia replaced the submarine service of World War II as the glamor boys of modern warfare.

In reality they made some serious mistakes that need to be explained in order to understand the direction, and even the outcome, of the war. First of all, they seemed committed to the idea, held by many Americans, that communism was a monolithic ideology and that by watching Moscow you were watching the communist world. Most still believed the worldwide ideology was being directed by the Soviet Union (Stalin) to the point that nothing was going to happen in Europe, or Asia or Africa, without Soviet involvement and permission. This was a serious mistake, as easily illustrated by a memo recently released that had been sent just prior to the North Korean invasion. In it the CIA described North Korea as "a firmly controlled Soviet satellite that exercised no independent initiative and depended entirely on the support of the USSR for its existence."[37] Looking back, explained one CIA historian Clayton Laurie, the agency should have considered North Korea on its own merit.

As it turned out, the North Korean invasion in June 1950 came as a surprise to the CIA. A recently declassified memorandum from January 13, 1950, showed the CIA did not understand what was happening in North Korea in the months leading up to the war. This memo takes note of the gradual movement toward the southwest taking place in the Korean Army, but interpreted this as "probably a defensive measure to offset the growing strength of the offensively minded south."[38] Only after the attack did the CIA acknowledge that the North Korean troops were far superior in numbers and weapons than they believed at first.

Truman, who had placed trust in the CIA, was so disgusted with them he replaced the director. In anticipation of more effective service from the agency, he charged it with determining the Chinese and Russian intentions when it came to Korea. Uninformed and often unaware, Washington felt it was walking a tightrope while the potential involvement of these two powers remained unknown. Intelligence was essential. The initial CIA report concluded that while both nations were perfectly capable of launching an attack, the agency saw no reason to believe that they would do so. Once again the CIA was focusing its intention on Europe, unaware of the strong nationalism present in North Korea.

Somehow the CIA did not detect the accumulation of two Chinese Army groups crossing into North Korea. They completely misread China, and in a top-secret report for the White House on October 12, 1950, after the first Chinese volunteers had crossed the Yalu, they still could not provide any "convincing indication" that a Chinese intervention was forthcoming. It was not until after Chinese infantrymen were taken prisoner and interrogated by local commanders that the CIA acknowledged that the communists had been moving south for months. Either the data was not there or the analysis failed to understand it. What little information was coming through was often wrong, and the overall appreciation for the situation unfounded. The CIA, for example, reported that the Chinese military, which had just fought a long and successful civil war, was poorly prepared, badly trained and underequipped.

Much is left to try to understand how the agency could have been so misinformed. Even when the Chinese played their hand and used the Indian ambassador to warn the United States not to cross the 38th parallel, nothing happened. China simply stated what they were going to do and then they did it. We need to be careful not to read our *post facto* knowledge into the situation, but every evidence is that the Chinese were serious and, more important, perfectly capable of doing just what they threatened. Some critics have suggested that the CIA, unable to understand Chinese thinking, misread the accumulating reasons for fighting a war with the United States.

So why is the CIA remembered as such a successful agency when it was so significantly unsuccessful? The answer is found in a combination of silence and propaganda. Vast amounts of the information pertaining to this intelligence-gathering service are held in such secrecy that "if they told us anything they would have to kill us." Nearly seventy years later, much of this is still classified, and a good deal of what has been reported by participants is both uninformative—meaning it talks more about organization than activities—and unreliable, meaning it cannot be trusted.[39] The highly successful propaganda campaign speaks for itself.

As it turned out, their more successful missions, though even this is questionable, were the agencies organized to conduct, and participate in, shadow activities. The CIA leadership was far more interested in "dirty tricks" than it was in the hardcore work of intelligence gathering. Those in Korea during the war saw themselves, and the partisan groups they led, as fighting men rather than agents of investigation. Some degree of this concern can be found in Ben Malcolm's postwar effort to get himself awarded the Combat Infantryman Badge. Malcolm claimed to be a CIA agent, and as such the army did not feel he was qualified. It was, Malcolm felt, an effort by the army bureaucracy to downplay what had been accomplished by those who served in special operations and unconventional warfare jobs in Korea.[40] It was, at the most, evidence of the confusion of assignment the military faced at the time.

Admittedly it is very hard for a Westerner to conduct behind-the-lines work in an Asian country. So most of the actual involvement was accomplished by men and women from North Korea who had fled from their homes in the face of the enemy. As agents they were brave and determined, but not well trained nor totally reliable.

Having failed twice to determine major enemy action, the agency nevertheless began to grow, and focused on clandestine operations conducted primarily by American-trained partisans. The activities, supported by the U.S. Air Force, expanded, and numerous guerrilla groups moved into North Korea to rescue pilots, conduct sabotage, and disrupt transportation.[41] By the time the war ended, the CIA was six times larger than it had been at the start. As its budget expanded, qualified personnel were recruited, and under the dynamic leadership of men like Allen W. Dulles, attention was given to "rewriting the past" in such a manner as to advance the reputation, exaggerate the mystique, and suggest accomplishments like the patrician operations, that were never really that successful.[42] Despite the number of personal memoirs that have appeared by self-identified agents, the CIA did not make much of a contribution.

The Soldiers Were Less Than Perfect

For the hard-nosed American pragmatist as well as the defensive military institution, the job in Korea had not been successfully accomplished. While defeat had been avoided, victory had not been achieved. In the minds of many, there was only one explanation: the GI had not performed as the American public had anticipated and expected he would. The elephant in the room for these returning young men and women was the stinging suspicion on the part of the nation that they had somehow failed. Among themselves, there was the suspicion they had not done the job they were sent to do.

The idea was not so much believed as it was felt. And while not often spoken of, it was expressed in a variety of other ways. The joy was dampened and the celebration somewhat curtailed because most Americans did not really know what had happened nor did they really know how to react.

In the building of this myth, the confusion of facts was assumed and the public reaction predictable. The word was out: Some of these young men returning to America had betrayed the nation. All who returned were stained by droppings from the same brush. Young Americans who had been sent off as warriors in a moral cause, to fight a primitive peasant army in a backward nation, had failed to perform with the same evidence of courage and diligence displayed by their fathers and older brothers in World War II.

Some who remembered were still influenced by the reporting of Maggie Higgins, the feisty young female correspondent whose early accounts claimed American soldiers often threw down their weapons and ran. That these Japanese occupation troops, flung into a major battle unprepared, had feigned sickness or injury to get out of combat. In some cases, particularly in the first few encounters with the enemy, this was sometimes the case. But it hardly reflected on the service provided, the sustained courage displayed, and the successful deployment as Allied forces increased.

David McConnell, a war correspondent for the *New York Herald*, said he had witnessed the confusion at the early part of the war and was astonished at what he considered the American weakness. He would write, "There is something wrong with American boys today. He won't fight. He gladly takes a whipping. Thinking only of running away. In my day I might have taken a whipping in a fight or a baseball game, but always scrapped back. These boys are weak."[43]

Unfortunately, many of these stories were spread by the military itself, seeking explanations for what was happening, and by the press in need of stories. Generals are good at misdirection and government is well-versed at avoiding blame, and the GI is an easy target to explain some of the unpleasantness. What was faced by these young men during the first months of the war was almost beyond imagination, and they had been poorly prepared for it. "We did our best, but look at what you sent to us to fight with. We were at first ill-prepared and poorly equipped but never lacked courage," complained a young staff officer still fighting a fear of failure some sixty years later.[44]

For lack of better words, it was suggested that the American soldier in Korea lacked the strength of character that the situation called for and, worse, that most POWs lacked courage. For many reasons, but to a significant degree in an effort to soften the failure to achieve victory, the blame was shifted away from the government that programmed the war, the military leadership who commanded it, and placed on the back of the GI "who failed to achieve it."

The stories were widespread; men were accused of deserting during battles, chastised for the inability or lack of willingness to accept hardship, and criticized for being outfought. Correspondent Higgins felt the need to tell the story at its worst. "So long as our government requires the backing of an aroused and informed public opinion it is necessary to tell the hard bruising truth. It is best to tell graphically the moments of desperation and horror endured by an unprepared army, so that the American public will demand that it never happen again."[45]

The problem, it was suggested by persons of considerable reputation and influence, was deep-seated and the fault could be laid at the feet of the mothers of the nation who had so babied their sons that they were no longer tough enough to be soldiers.[46]

The prisoners of war fared little better. When they were finally released, the first impression was that the breakdown among them had been nearly complete. The army organized massive psychological studies and instigated not only the conduct of the prisoners as a whole, but each and every one individually. The army finally concluded that as many as 425 men were in a position to be tried by court-marital for providing aid to the enemy. But for a variety of reasons, most unstated in the records, only 14 were actually put on trial. When they began, the trials were highly unpopular among the American people.

There was, of course, the added myths of brainwashing that exaggerated the suspicions and suggested a weakness, not only in the American troops, but among men and women in general that made them so vulnerable to the communists teachings. What, men and women asked themselves in the dark corners of their lives, can be done to defeat this enemy that has learned how to turn the hearts and minds of our warriors?

It is important to remember that at this time nearly every adult in America had gone through the Great Depression and World War II. They had met the challenge and were sure that America could withstand the global threats of communism as well as the fear of domestic weakness. So for many the "failure" in Korea was a crack in the wall. It was the first real test. It hung like a shadow over their sense of invincibility.

What's wrong with America and with the military that they could not defeat a local militia in a unknown country? No one knew of Korea and very little about China, and they were not highly regarded. How could these poor nations defeat the most powerful nation in the world? The cream of World War II generals could do nothing about it; they apparently had no solution. Those responsible for preserving our way of life had somehow allowed a war of no vital strategic or traditional interest to end in a deadlock. It was the kiss of death for national pride and memory. It was the curse of the veteran.

Somehow, it was often assumed, the communists had managed to wash the brains of Americans and replace the vacant spaces with a mistrust of country and a love of communism. This was accomplished in some unexplained magical manner that effected them all to some degree. The examples were most prevalent among the POWs, but the suspicion covered them all. As is the case with so many of these myths, there is little to suggest this is true. Most of these feelings had grown without justification, spread by media organizations often more interested in a story than reporting. The evidence is simply not there, and yet the attitude remained and continues to appear in books and articles now years after the end of the war: The American soldier was weak.

The military was as much responsible for this attitude as anyone, and many a general blamed the quality and preparation of the troops for their losses. They often joined with the American people, the media, and the government in allowing criticism to swing in this direction. If one stops for a moment to take a reality check, it becomes evident that most of these assumptions fail to hold up. Considering the number of men involved both in the war and as POWs, there is very little evidence of desertion, cowardliness, betrayal, collaboration, or even a change in their political orientations. A comparison of the World War II German POW camp with what was faced in Korea is simply irrational, and yet that has been the case.

So, asks the critic in search of evidence of weakness, why didn't the Americans try to escape from prison camps? Is it not the duty of every American soldier to avoid capture, and if captured to try to escape? The difficulty in trying to escape from imprisonment in a nation that is primarily foreign is magnified by the inability to mingle with the native citizens. This was the same problem faced by Americans held captive in Japan during World War II. It is hardly evidence of weakness.

This false understanding has never really been cleared up, and one see hints of it in many contemporary histories. Current responses to Korean veterans do not seem to maintain this feeling, though you still find it expressed particularly by World War II veterans hanging about the American Legion centers. In most cases it was not something you talked about. But unfortunately a lot of the veterans themselves carry it with them: "Why weren't we good enough?" We will discuss it later, but the primary difference between the behavior of World War II POWs and Korean War POWs is to be found in the prison, not in the prisoner.

Any sort of comparison between soldiers of different wars will fail because of the vast differences in both wars and soldiers. Who is to say, and on what basis do you determine, that the militiaman at Bunker (Breed's) Hill was braver than the young Marine at Hamburger Hill, or the enlisted reservist on Omaha Beach better than the amphibious soldier at Wonsan? But when looking at the accounts of America's many wars, it is hard not to be struck by the fact that what is different about the memory of the behavior of the soldier is to found in the nature of the question that is being asked.

The U.S. Used Biological Weapons

As a propaganda effort, the communist campaign to cast blame on the United States for the use of biological weapons was a success. It caused considerable harm to the American image. It was picked up and generally believed in Asia and was significant in Europe where it disturbed our NATO partners. The avid denials provided by the Americans were weakened by the country's long and well-known interest in biological weapons. And, of course, by the degree to which we captured and built upon the Japanese program at the end of World War II. Both China and the Soviet Union were aware of experimental labs in the United States that were working on the development of such weapons. The charge was simple and effective: the United States was utilizing germ warfare in Korea.

While there had been earlier charges that the United States was introducing smallpox into Korea, it was not until mid–February of 1952 that the Soviet radio accused the U.S. of dropping insects, rats, and chicken feathers in order to spread disease among enemy troops. The communists had been able to obtain and publish a series of confessions from downed pilots that admitted that they had participated in such activities. The charge was provided some validity by the fact that at one time former Secretary of Defense Louis Johnson acknowledged that the United States had such weapons and could use them in Korea if it became necessary.[47]

The underlying value to the communists, other than the propaganda image of the United States, was as a cover-up for the harsh medical conditions in North Korea and China, and to draw attention away from the unrest that this caused. During the war, the civilian medical services had pretty much collapsed, and the rapid movement of troops and refugees distributed disease at an alarming rate. There was no doubt that sickness was a significant problem for the Koreans. And someone made the connection.

The claims and the evidence presented were persuasive and hard to deny. Among those who considered the accusations legitimate was the revisionist historian Jon Halliday, who in the 1980s, along with Gavan McCormack, provided what they thought was good evidence. However, it was not until 1999 that investigative authors Stephen Endicott and Edward Hagerman went to press with the claim that the U.S.

46

did in fact use biological weapons in Korea during the war. Conrad Crans, writing for the Air Force, supported the idea with evidence he said showed American pilots were involved.[48] Lieutenant Kenneth Enoch, who confessed that planes from his 3rd Bomber Wing had dropped germ-laden artifacts over North Korean villages, did not, on his return home, recant. His confession is on display at the Victorious Fatherland Museum in Korea. Ryall reports that the records of Lieutenant Enoch's flight over North Korea on the dates in question were removed from the official record shortly after his confession appeared.[49]

The British scientist Joseph Needham said that he had found evidence that the charges were true. He quoted, among other things, confessions by American POWs who claimed firsthand knowledge. There is one bit of evidence about germ warfare that seem irrefutable and suggests an attitude about the use of germs. At one time General Ridgway asked whether, if at the last moment he was not able to stop the Chinese advance, he could use germ warfare. General MacArthur said no.[50]

Interestingly enough, it was the Russian archive that provided the best information, first showing how the charges might be used in the internal fight for control after the death of Stalin. Kathryn Weathersby, in searching the Soviet archive, was able to provide documentation that the charges were not true and that they had been set up by China and North Korea without Russian knowledge. She indicated that the evidence placed before world opinion was in fact manufactured by the communists and that Russia passed it along only as long as they believed it was true. It was only after the Russians became aware of their illegitimacy that the charges died down.[51] In April 1953 the Soviets, in memos, apparently acknowledged the fact there was no biological warfare in North Korea. It now appears that as early as May 1953 the Russians knew it was a hoax and ended the charges, and said China had misrepresented the situation. The Russian government suggested that the charges be dropped and that no Soviet who was working in Korea continue supporting the idea.

It is hard to believe that Russia could have been as unaware of the plot as it suggests. Some continue to believe they had been a part of the plan and had manufactured evidence to be used in supporting the idea.[52] Laurent Beria, in charge of Soviet Intelligence during this period, left documents that suggested thousands were involved in creating the file of evidence used to support this medical fraud.

Much of the discussion about the use of biological warfare in Korea has calmed down since the war and has become more of an academic football than a public issue. The dubious nature of much of the evidence presented in support of the communist claims prevents any answer to be considered final. On the other hand, half-truths made by America in many of its explanations make it difficult to believe there was not something going on. As informative as they have been, the Soviet documents may suggest they were not a part of planning the hoax, but they did little to stop it.

The suggestion that germ warfare was used by the United Nations during the Korean War remains in the mythology. With so much smoke around, many cannot help but feel there was a fire someplace. It may never be proved to anyone's satisfaction one way or the other. But this much is true beyond a reasonable doubt: while the military may not have used germ warfare in Korea, they provided every evidence that they were willing to do so.

A Successful Armistice Was Achieved

The generally accepted belief is that the fighting in Korea ended with negotiations that, for the most part, were seen as legitimate and reasonably successful. This is not the case at hand. However, weak and confused as they are, they have managed to prevent rekindling the flame of war and provided a peace of sorts for three-quarters of a century. This period has allowed South Korea to expand and emerge as a powerful nation among the family of nations. It has allowed the two Koreas to live side by side. It does not seem to matter that the Republic of (South) Korea never signed the agreement and does not feel compelled to pay it much homage.

There does not seem to be a lot of information available about the agreement, and it is doubtful if other than a few international lawyers and academics have ever read it. There is little realization that the primary contribution it makes is not what it says but that it exists at all. Its value lies only in its symbolic suggestion of peace, not in what it calls for or has produced. The armistice is primarily a failure. That is, it was designed in such a way that it was bound to fail.[53]

Such a failure was destined, if for no other reason than to acknowledge that the armistice talks were military, not political or diplomatic.

In these discussions the meaningful language of diplomacy was inappropriate and ineffective—it did not mean the same thing to all involved. Even the ignorance of their respective languages made it necessary for the delegations to give undue attention to the gestures and nonverbal behavior of their opponents. Both sides finally resorted to using interpreters from the field hospitals, because they had the best chance of being neutral.[54] In the extension of these talks, the communist assigned experienced political leaders to their delegations and sought a long-term political advantage from them, while the United Nations reverted to military men with no experience or training, seeking a cease-fire, and who "deeply distrusted their adversaries."[55]

The significant question that hovered over the talks concerned the questions of reunification for one, and economic stability for the other. These were not addressed with any seriousness. The most prominent of these questions, reunification, was put off, postponed for future talks to be accomplished in formal and official meetings of international leaders. The critical meeting took place on one occasion but never again. The agreement, despite all its signatures, did not establish rules for the relationship between the two Koreas, one of which did not sign it, and made no provisions for the abstract characteristics of the bodies involved.

Lyndon Johnson considered the cease-fire fraudulent. He believed that it would accomplish no purpose other than to allow the enemy to release its aggressive armies someplace else.

IV

Failed Expectations

> Life is so constructed that the event does not, cannot,
> will not, match the expectation.—*Charlotte Brontë*

Time has done little to ease the discomfort of the Korean veterans for whom the war continues to be a problem, other perhaps than to distance them somewhat from the causes of their unrest. Part of it, of course, is that they came home with some expectations of appreciation—some expressions in keeping with the wide acceptance of the Greatest Generation—and that has not worked out. The national response has been less than expected. But more important to the GI is that much of the response appears to be tainted with a certain reluctance to act at all. The veteran had felt this lack of interest in a response and saw the halfhearted efforts feeling somehow they were being damned by faint praise. It was, as Lieutenant John Schultz would suggest after several years, "as if the nation could not decide if they wanted to let us back or not."[1]

While some expectations may well have been unrealistic, they were nevertheless serious. Paradoxically the veterans retained little faith that the army would do what they promised, or that the government had any sense of commitment. Perhaps they should have returned with their eyes open; perhaps they should have expected nothing more.

The fighting men knew they could not all come home as heroes. But surely the nation would be glad to see them, at least to acknowledge that they had been gone. Maybe there would be parades along the same streets of American cities as their fathers and brothers had experienced. The veterans, marching with their units displaying banners and medals, and basking in thanksgiving, accepting the nation's applause. But there was never any discussion of a national response. Few parades. Certainly some home towns came out to greet the local hero and the veteran was once in a while invited to speak to the Chamber of Commerce. Occasionally a local paper would announce the return. But no outpouring of national pride and its accompanying ticker-tape emerged. After all this time one might think it would be forgotten, but it is not, and the veteran speaks of the lack of celebration with a sad regret. There were, metaphorically, no yellow ribbons around the old oak tree.

While it was evident that the world had carried on without them, they were most acutely aware that their lives had been delayed. The veterans of this war drifted home and back into society as easily as they could. Most, at that time, were required to remain in the reserves for seven years, so the military was never far behind. They went back to their families, to their jobs, to participation in activities, and to assume their responsibilities. They sought to re-enter their communities. They tried to pay little attention to the sense of excitement that was missing, and the gap that appeared between them and those who made up their world.

They did not know what, or even how, but things had changed. The old job was not the same as it was when they left; the old pleasures had lost most of their taste, earlier activities lacked in luster previously felt. Many of the people they remembered were no longer the same people as when they left and they had nothing to say; old conversations had dried up. Most realized that something was different, but they were not sure what it was. As one cliché puts it, "We left to the sounds of Les Brown and came home to the music of Elvis Presley."

One of the things most veterans anticipated was an emerging sense of status; a sense that they were coming home with a new level of acceptance. They were now different. They were now representatives of that long line of proud troops who had for centuries responded to the nation's call. They were a part of a tradition. And with some potential pride they anticipated belonging to that elite group of men and women who had stood tall in the service of their country. There would be a new respect, a new identity, that would unite them, if not politically and in associations, at least emotionally with the best in the country. That much they expected, but that is not how it was. The change in status was, many reported, not the wearing of a new mantle of respectability, but rather of difference, of isolation. They were seen as being different, but not in the manner they had anticipated.

The sense of isolation was, of course, a carryover from the individualism of the battlefield. In this case, it was very much the product of a different military process. When the military decided to organize the 8th Army in Korea around the individual soldier rather than units, the pipeline of replacements moving overseas did so as individuals, not units. Once the soldier arrived, he was somewhat arbitrarily assigned to a unit, and then moved about indiscriminately for the good of the service. This type of deployment limited the possibilities for long term attachment to comrades and unit pride.

When the time came to come home, the system was reversed, and they came home as individuals, in many cases as one man on a boatload of soldiers who had never been together before. There was almost no unit identification or connection, no brothers-in-arms forged over years together, no long regimental pride with which to associate. Most of these men came home as they had left: one man lost in a gigantic industry of interchangeable parts.

Most of these tough young men were not so misguided as to believe that the hero always got his due, but they did expect to be recognized once they had rejoined the population. They expected some admiration, maybe even love, or lacking that, at least respect or pride. Some sense of intimacy with those for whom they had fought; a role they had played in the expectations of the nation. This was generally not the case. There are few cases of veterans being harassed, or spit on, or attacked in public places, as was the case for some Vietnam veterans. But there was also little respect. It was not there. At least it was not manifest, as the veteran might have imagined. "Wearing my uniform to church the day after returning from Korea I found that I was more the elephant in the room than the object of attention; a man of mission and purpose."[2]

At the very least, the veteran returned with the expectation of benefits equal to, and perhaps even surpassing, those received by other veterans. Benefits promised and earned with honor and designed to compensate for time lost, for income disrupted, and to help get started again. And while the benefits came, they did so with a strange reluctance, and they were less generous and with many more restrictions than previous plans. There was considerable opposition, including an inquiry as to their validity called up by President Eisenhower, who himself felt that military service was an "obligation of citizenship" and not the basis for benefits. Some basic differences were most notable: Korea provided no unemployment compensation for those just out of the service, the Korean plan paid the GI a monthly payment for education rather than paying university tuition as after World War II, waiting times were extended, and access to the VA programs harder to get.

Even in death, the Korean veterans' graves were scattered about the country, as there are no dedicated spots for those who fell in that war. The Korean veteran is often buried alone. The military, aware that the nature of the war in Korea meant they could not guarantee holding on to a particular piece of land, decided against military cemeteries. The bodies of the dead would be shipped home, but not to national cemeteries. To the largest extent they were sent to their home town, where the fallen soldier's body was laid to rest among decades of previous inhabitants. Those few who ended up at Arlington or one of the national cemeteries were given headstones that listed name, rank, and date of birth and death. No mention of the war. A few years later, after considerable pressure from families who complained about the lack of recognition of the cause for which their loved one died, the Department of Defense authorized the inclusion of "Korea." Nothing more.

A part of this continued sense of being "outside" has been the veterans' awareness of the lack of national interest, or even press coverage, of the investment they made. As events unfolded in Korea over the years, there has been very little national awareness or connection with the earlier effort seen. Years of conflict, border disputes, deaths, and continued violence have been little noticed. Even during a period of clashes known as the "Second Korean War," the veterans were barely commented on, making little to no connection between what had happened a decade before and what was going on.

The veterans' passing years have also been effected by a number of things they did not expect to encounter. Some of these were the result of the nation's behavior, some primarily a result of their own miscalculations. There was no particular thing that stands out as evidence the Korean veteran might be considered "less a veteran," or as they often said, "chopped liver." Certainly there was no reason to believe that anyone, or any group, was trying to discredit or mistreat those who had served. It was not that. It was the continuing accumulation of limited response that was soon seen as evidence that the nation, or its leaders, viewed them in a less significant light than they had veterans from the previous war. In addition to the array of lesser considerations, they were surprised by some things that they discovered. These social and economic slights were joined by overt acts that played out a far more serious role.

They did not expect to see the nation so unaffected by a war that had so touched them. It did not go unnoticed that when they returned there was little evidence available that suggested the people at home were involved in the same war. No signs that the war had cost them anything. Despite attempts to encourage it, families never got around to displaying the star in the window that told the world they were the proud parents of an active duty soldier. It had been important in previous wars to let those passing know someone in the house was in the military. Little such pride was displayed among Americans in the 1950s.

They did not expect to uncover the myth of defeat, even of cowardliness, that apparently haunted their acceptance. It was rarely if ever displayed on a personal basis, but existed in the background as a discussion, primarily between the military and academics, about what had happened. Little in this daunting literature ever fully discussed if in fact the American soldier in Korea was weaker, more cowardly, less loyal, or less capable than was the case in other wars. Rather, the discussion was carried on in the veteran's presence but not with his participation—like your mother discussing your faults with your aunt while you are in the room. The cloud was there. The suspicion was there. There was always the question: Why had the soldiers not measured up?

They did not expect to be as silent about their service as they turned out to be. Those who served in both World War II and Korea preferred to list themselves as veterans of the earlier war. The Korean War veteran rarely wore pieces of old uniforms, or badges, or combat fatigues, and only in the last decade has the "I am a Korean veteran" hat shown up. Few put POW on their license plates; it created too many questions.

They did not expect to be betrayed. Nevertheless, the betrayal exposed the deliberate disengagement in government behavior that lay bare the real lack of concern about those involved in the war. Of primary concern was the treatment of prisoners of war (POWs). These men who had been taken prisoner were the subject of endless discussions, planning, and political maneuvering, but in the end they were not treated as they deserved to be. Nor were they protected by the very government that they had been imprisoned while defending. They had been mistreated, disrespected at a time when the nation could have chosen to do otherwise.

As time passed, doubt was replaced and suspicion confirmed that the American government had failed to keep the primary promise made to those being sent off to war: No man shall be left behind. This apparently was only a slogan. Those who were responsible for the failure to do so were, years later, still in the upper levels of government, their crimes hidden in the shadows of misinformation.[3] The increasing knowledge of the covert behavior, and of any significant protests executed by veterans, has been manipulated rather than acknowledged and adds fuel to the fire of disillusionment. Have I been sleeping with the enemy?

In an effort to correct the situation, but certainly in no way to compensate for it, the government has spent millions of dollars of public funds trying to locate bodies of those left behind. Yet at the same time they continue to deny it ever happened. This nearly implausible effort that Colonel Millard Peck called "the illusion of progress through hyperactivity" fails to correct or justify the situation. Is it any wonder that a good many veterans are coming to believe that someone in the government, or even the government as some sort of acting agent, did not want those prisoners to come home?[4] The evidence is overwhelming that President Eisenhower personally authorized the signing of an armistice with the enemy, knowing full well that American prisoners-of-war were still being held by the communists in China and Russia.

Fearing some sort of unwanted delay in the peace agreement, the government decided to ignore the fact that a significant number of men were still being held and that the hard-fought agreement about the full exchange of prisoners had not been followed. By this time their fate has most likely already been settled, but their absence from the roll of prisoners lost and then returned makes a much larger noise in the silence. It does not soften what was done, nor does it explain why it was allowed.

Politically right or wrong? A militarily necessity?[5] It makes little difference. The distrust left by such a reality rests like a dormant infection and adds to the semi-fatalism with which the Korean War soldier dealt with so many unexplained or unexpected events. An attitude of wait and see. The acceptance that now, at this time, what has happened makes little difference to anyone. Whatever!

"Whatever," they said, but what did they mean? It does not mean that it does not matter. Rather it is a statement of defeat, of the realization they are going to have to live with what has happened, that there is nothing they can do about it, they can only determine how they will respond. If the hot food trucks failed to arrive as promised, or the long-anticipated showers were never available, or the quick retreat from an enemy advance led them into a trap, all were dealt with in the same fashion: "Whatever." Sometimes it was the philosophical acceptance summed up in that other popular expression among Korean soldiers: "That is the way the ball bounces." But it still is a moral crime.

Nor did the returning veteran expect to feel hints of shame and defilement. For some, involvement in a war is a game, but it is a game of the greatest significance. The experience of such participation is for many persons the only real opportunity to expose and explore those regions of the human psyche which, without such an experience, will always remain uncharted.[6] Whether challenged or not, the human soul seems to possess this shadow of a doubt about their own stamina, about how much they can take, and whether, when the final bell is sounded, they can prevail. The true meaning of manhood—not necessarily restricted to men—is some final evidence of individual courage that has been tested in the presence of extreme violence. Nations may feel this way as well, believing that the red badge of courage is the only real evidence of their credibility. But if this be the case, then one must consider the impact on the nations—as it would the impact on the individual—when they fail to measure up. This limited war to contain communism had far more at stake, and so far has not been seen as an positive step in the care and feeding a our national soul.

The Vietnam veteran is often identified by his anger. The general character of this anger is found in a belief they had fought an unnecessary war against an unanticipated enemy, leading to an unwanted conclusion. The distinct character of the anger is more often located in the confusion of meaning that accompanied their memory of service. This feeling, as yet only poorly identified, nevertheless appeared in Korea as well and among the Korean servicemen. The existence of this feeling, more a matter of sadness in the Korean veteran, would appear to be as much a feeling as it is a conviction, and thus is perhaps only a suspicion. But the lack of concrete evidence to explain it is somewhat offset by the reflections of sensitive men and women who for years have reflected on its awareness.

One man seems to come the closest to providing an identity and perhaps some insight. W. Taylor Stevenson, a highly respected theologian, suggested that "the [Korean] veteran suffers from a sense of defilement—a belief that he had been dishonored and symbolically dirtied by the breakdown of taboos that protected America's sense of innocence and powerfulness."[7]

Expressed in a variety of ways from shame to mistrust, many Korean veterans have voiced their uneasiness about their involvement in the war and what, unlike service in the world wars, caught them unprepared to accept the pride of their accomplishment. Their concern was not so much with themselves as individuals as it was with the war itself. That the nation had acted in a manner that they, as individuals, would not have acted. That their country had used them as tools in an immoral process. They encountered the distressing hint that America had placed them in a situation that was primarily in violation of the nation's moral interests and had made them a party to actions beneath the dignity of the nation's long tradition. Their call to service was unheralded in its lack of necessity and placed them in a war so lacking in any heritage of honor and justice that it forever left them scarred by the experience.[8]

In a variety of ways, the veterans are suspicious that in the name of patriotism and as a call of community service, they had been placed in the midst of a situation that was not necessary to preserve freedom, or save the world for democracy, or even to stop the growth of the communist disease. Rather, they had been sent to war for the sake of war, and they came away from the experience soiled. They suspected that, for the first time in modern history—at least in American history—the moral justification for military involvement was ignored, and that in their ignorance, or perhaps only their innocence, they had been violated by the shame. A shame perhaps different from simple guilt—but seen in withdrawal, in hiding, and in secrets and silence—a disappointment within ourselves about ourselves.

V

Memory Mistakes
Minimize Mission

Silence is a lie that screams at the light.
—*Shannon Adler*

Childhood, some wise person once observed, is a period in which you have to listen to adults tell you things you already know. Such a view described the situation the veteran sometimes feels when he hears bad information provided by those who do not know any better. This is particularly true of data that is primarily more myth than fact. A seemingly endless number of persons, including some otherwise respected novelists and historians, have become so attached to the myths emerging from the Korean War that it is little wonder there is difficulty in knowing what to remember. Recently solid historians like Dr. James Matray as well as some emerging revisionists have begun to address some of these issues, but unfortunately there are still works emerging, lectures given, and classes taught with the old stories still intact. The unfounded acceptance of these myths prevents the understanding and appreciation of what actually happened, and more important, what the reality of the information has to teach us.

Lacking a specific goal when committing ourselves to the war, and having fought it without any identifiable justification, as well as seeing it end without closure, all provided grounds for the emergence of a series of explanations that grew to meet the needs of the moment. All wars have their stories and traditions that extrapolate and expound on events, seeking to leave a good taste behind despite the desperation of the reality. Maybe the Korean War is no worse than the rest of them. But it seems overwhelmed by the acceptance of myths that in the long run prevent understanding of or appreciation for what happened.

Today much of the story we tell ourselves has lost its context and we are awash with inconsistency and paradox. There is an incredible amount of misinformation circulated. Some of it was propaganda created by an embarrassed military; some was misinformation spread by an administration under fire; some consists of assumptions drawn from lack of information; and some is the result of direct, deliberate, and bold-faced lies. A few examples will quickly identify the problem.

The Hordes

If you read Korean military history, especially memoirs or unit histories, you will have run into a statement like this many times: "Vastly outnumbered, we fought off the hordes of Chinese that attacked in waves." Other terms that are used include human wave or human sea attacks. The veteran is inclined to ask, "How many Chinese does it take to make a horde?"

The myth of this attack method, as well as the assumption of overwhelming superiority of numbers, has prevailed since the first days of the war, and it became the easy excuse to explain failures on the battlefield. What is clear is that the communists enjoyed overwhelming numerical support only in the opening state of the conflict and during the initial incursion of the Chinese. In most cases the United States and South Korean forces actually outnumbered their enemy, sometimes by a ratio of two to one. Surprise, better discipline and better weapons (the Russian T-34 tank, for example) gave the North Koreans an advantage.

Looking first at the assumption of waves, it needs to be understood that if you are in a fixed position, a bunker perhaps, and the enemy keeps attacking your point over and over again, you are going to be inclined to consider it a wave attack and to make the unjustified assumption that it is maintained along a wide battle front. That was not the case. The communist forces' attacks were adapted from the Japanese Banzai, practiced as early as the 1920s. It works like this. A particular and previously selected spot on the enemy line is identified. Your troops focus on the spot, which might well be only a hundred yards wide. Then you attack along this very narrow front and never stop coming. You do not allow any lulls in the battle. It is in this point of concentration that the communist forces were successful. Once they attacked, they would continue to focus on that point until the enemy line either broke or they ran out of men.

As for being outnumbered, the fact is that with the exception of the first 45 days or so, the United Nations troops in the Korean War were not outnumbered. When the first communist troops crossed the line, the United States had little more than 500 advisors on call, and the South Korean Army was primarily on "harvest leave." The tide quickly changed as troops were brought first from Japan and then from the States. Even when the Chinese forces entered the war, the number of communist troops was not a significant factor. The failure to achieve a military success is made even more difficult to explain when acknowledging the UN had more men on the ground and more equipment in the air and more ships on the water than did the enemy we faced.

There is no doubt that the military was unprepared for the well-trained, combat-experienced masses of men that pushed forward into the Republic of (South) Korea. And while the initial invasion, the fall of Seoul, and the retreat toward the small port city of Pusan were accomplished by a superior number of enemy troops, it did not continue to be the case. Nevertheless, the belief has maintained that this was the situation throughout the war. Such an assumption distorts any understanding of the fighting that took place, misleads those who would learn strategy, and denies the impact of logistics. And yet the belief persists, particularly in memoirs, unit histories, and popular history. The belief prevails that the massive manpower-rich Chinese and North Korean armies were victorious by overpowering and overwhelming the defenders. "Massive waves of communist fighters" became the estimate when exact figures were not known. The truth is, however, that during most of the war, while some North Korean and Chinese forces did attack in massive fronts, it was not the common strategy.

As we learn more and more about the war, it becomes somewhat obvious that the North Koreans and the Chinese made as much, or more, use of the tactic of infiltration, and that it was this, not waves, that gave our troops the most pain. In the long run, however, what made the communist soldier so much stronger in the minds of their leaders was their high spirits, superior morale sustained by the party's relentless political domination, and indoctrination. The Allies, expecting a small, weak peasant army, were shocked at the vitality of its enemy, but it was not numbers, but modern strategic leadership, that was primarily its strong point.

The Marines Won the War

The number of places you see this referred to, and the widespread belief orchestrated by the Marine Corps and its friends, has made this the standard identity. Literally dozens of books and articles are written on this assumption. One form or the other of the phrase "the Marines won the war and saved the Army and South Korea from destruction" appears. T.R. Fehrenbach's early work provides such a view,[1] and Faris Kirtland, writing in the *Armed Forces and Society Journal*, is such an example.[2] While the U.S. Marines are a fine fighting force, and due much credit for their traditional involvement in the defense of the nation, they did not earn this particular distinction.

Some scholars suggest the Marines enjoyed greater success than the army in Korea because men in command positions had been trained in combat, unlike many of the Army officers, who had moved up the chain of command without any particular combat experience. Certainly rules of training, the volunteer nature of the Corps, the exaggerated spirit of the Corps, and opportunity, all related to the fact that the Marines responded when called and performed a great service. So great that some authors, in believing the Marines did it all, use the term "Marine" to mean all military personnel. John Goulden, in his excellent history of the war, gives this impression several times, in one case calling his chapter on Inchon "Marines Hit the Beaches." The Corps played an important part but it did not however, justify the bogus accumulation of wealth for which they have become so popular.[3]

The statement about the Marines' winning the Korean War is not only false; it is not even remotely true. The more legitimate understanding of their situation would be that the Korean War probably saved the U.S. Marines, which at the time were under fire from the Congress and the other services and were targeted for extinction. President Truman disliked the Marines, and the other services referred to them as "the navy's army." Congress, with its eye on postwar budgets, wanted to phase them out. As it turned out, their contribution to the war, real and imagined, provided them support when they dearly needed it. Somehow they convinced America that victory was dependent on their involvement. The pre-planned and perpetuated myths of Marine success, even at the expense of the other services, has done a great disservice to the thousands of men and women—primarily infantrymen from more than twenty-five other nations—who carried the brunt of the war.

Simply as a matter of fact, and despite their widespread claims, the Marines were not the first United States forces in Korea. No, the first was an antiaircraft unit sent to defend the evacuation, and then follow-up segments of the U.S. Army's 7th Division arrived. Nor were the Marines the only ones to drive the enemy from the Pusan perimeter. Rather, after taking part in the 8th Army push out of Pusan and their drive east and north, the Marines were pulled off battle for the perimeter and sent to take part in the attack on Inchon. At this point the 8th Army moved the enemy north until they joined the Marines at Inchon and on the way to Seoul. At that point the question of supply lines became moot.[4] No, they were not the only ones at Inchon, as suggested by the encyclopedia chronology of the war: "7th Marines land on Korean west coast and secure their objective."[5]

No, they were not the only ones making sea landing on the Korean coast; in fact, they were not the first. The Second Cavalry Division landed (administratively) successfully before entering the battle at the Pusan Perimeter. No, the Marines were not the only units cut off by the Chinese. Nor were they the only ones involved in the fighting withdrawal during the long retreat from the Chinese at Chosin. General Smith, the Marine commander, always forgot to mention the 31st Regiment or the 3rd Division that held the enemy back, making it possible for the Marines to disembark and sail away. When the time came, the general refused to recommend Army outfits for unit citations.[6]

In the execution of this war, the United States provided well over 90 percent of the equipment and at least that percentage of the non-Korean troops fighting the war. But the United States did not supply all the troops, nor all the equipment, nor pay all the costs. Among those who need to be remembered are the troops from some twenty-six nations, some as large as Great Britain and some as small Luxembourg, who sent their own marines to do battle.

The war was not fought only by Marines, nor were they responsible for the victory, such as it was. That is equally true for the Air

Force, which is still claiming that their involvement was more essential than it was. In terms of numbers, both involved and casualties, the Army fought the Korean War. The Air Force, the Navy, the Coast Guard, the Marines, the Army Nurse Corps, and even the Merchant Marine played highly significant parts, but it was the Army that fought the war. Interservice rivalry, endorsed by some overly biased historians and Marine Corps policies, have suggested otherwise, and this is a part of the betrayal veterans have experienced.

Known primarily as amphibious troops, Marines nevertheless fought much of their war in Korea as infantry assigned to 8th Army. The scoreboard for the Marines can only be identified as mixed. While they did well at those significant moments so well recorded—Pusan, Inchon, Seoul, Chosin Reservoir—they were no more than adequate infantry soldiers when put on the line with the rest of the United Nations troops. Marine Corps Commandant General Clifton B. Cates, sensing the array of forces fighting to dismantle the Marines, talked General MacArthur into requesting a Marine Regimental Combat Team and eventually a division. An RCT, pulled together from reservists and scattered Marines on embassy duty, arrived at Pusan without equipment, wearing their distinctive camouflaged helmet covers and yellow shin leggings, and moving with characteristic swagger.[7] Their arrival and long and honorable service in Korea rekindled public and congressional support much needed during this period of military transition.[8]

The Miracle at Inchon

While some historians like James Matray have begun to call these miracle myths into question, vast numbers of persons working in the field are still making the unsubstantiated assumptions that the landing at Inchon Harbor and the drastic defeat at Chosin Reservoir were military marvels worthy of great appreciation. Such is the memory, and it is a very cloudy memory at best. Hundreds of articles have been written about the invasion at Inchon, looking at it from a variety of directions, but most still based their comments on the genius of the effort without telling us exactly what that genius was. This assumption needs a more objective look.

The landing that took place on 15 September 1950 was a limited success, but not a miracle, and all the historical gushing about what happened there leads to a misreading of what was happening.

The primary key to the success at Inchon was not the limited military overpowering of the enemy's inadequate defenses, but the remarkable manner in which the Navy overcame the unpredictability of Flying Fish Channel.[9] On the other hand, the retreat of United States forces from the Chosin Reservoir, remembered with assumptions that cannot be supported, was rather a masterpiece of military stupidity and unpreparedness that has somehow become tragically heroic.

For a good many writing of this period, the events at Inchon have so overshadowed the other activities—say, the tough battle to drive the North Koreans from the Pusan and north—is ignored. Well respected historian James Gould considers the landing under the title "MacArthur's Manifest Exposition."[10] Gould was no fan of the general and described him as a "recalcitrant general who finally stepped over the borders of acceptable behavior in series of public statements."

This invasion was not nearly as risky as many histories have suggested, nor was it as daring as reported. The invasion behind the lines was a significant amphibious landing, but it was not a critical one. MacArthur was aware of the limited protection of the area and the massive effort he could put ashore. The biggest risk was logistics, but it was most certainly not beyond the capabilities that the combined services had provided him several times before. And while the landing did have the effect of cutting off the supply lines to the south, it is also a fact that by the time the attack reached Seoul and had proven successful in its mission, the Eighth Army had pushed its way north and the supply lines were no long a matter of significance. If history were true to the facts, it might well be discovered that the real heroes of the Inchon landing were the U.S. Navy and Merchant Marines for conquering the infamous demands and rampant dangers of Flying Fish Channel.[11]

Military historians like Spencer Tucker described the landing as a "brilliant success, carefully planned and flawlessly executed," and in doing so seem to reflect the most accepted point of view. Others, however, like Russell Stolfi in the article "Critique on Pure Reason," are not so sure, and agree that the main point of the landing was already accomplished with the Eighth Army's drive north.

All the talk about Inchon has, for example, led to a nearly complete disregard of a number of other invasion points and battles. It has as well led to the near total lack of appreciation and understanding of the many amphibious landings staged by the U.S. Army.[12] Take, for example, the initial early landing of the Cavalry Division just north of Pusan during the early days of the war. Or MacArthur's follow-up plan that called for a Marine landing at the east coast port city of Wonson. The First Marine and Seventh Army Divisions, hastily pulled out of the fighting at Seoul, were delivered to Pusan, from where they were to launch their invasion. The execution of the event can only be described as a farce, though its failure to work out as planned was hardly funny. Late arriving at Wonson, the Marine troopships found they could not disembark because the harbor was full of communist sea mines. As the field was cleared, the Marines sailed in circles for five days, around and around. When the danger was over, the Marines landed administratively (without enemy opposition) in an area taken days earlier by the advancing elements of the Republic of Korea army. The night before the Marine landing, Bob Hope entertained the troops.

Many called MacArthur the visionary general when they were discussing the landing. Perhaps, but he was also a man familiar with history, who was aware of Marquis de Montcalm's 1759 attack on Quebec during the French and Indian Wars, and of the successful landing of Marines at the same Inchon harbor a hundred years before the First Korean War.[13] The idea did not arrive full-blown in the general's head, nor were the methods for accomplishing it unknown.

The Victory at Chosin

The other shadow of this miracle memory is little other than a clearly defined case of denial. "Retreat Hell" is a fine slogan for the speaker at a motivational conference, but it is hardly a reasonable description of the greatest defeat and rout of military forces in American history: the Chinese advance from the Chosin Reservoir. This was a low point in the American tradition of war and was due "to paper planners and politicians, including MacArthur."[14]

Few have had the nerve to take on the bombardment of justifications and explanations for a military action that must certainly have been questionable in intent and impossibly led in execution. Martin

Ross, Marine turned writer, is as much to blame as anyone for a lot of this misinformation, and certainly must get prolonged credit for promoting the Marines during this time. But even Ross, in his works on the Korean War, admits that the Marine follow-up was to cover the army with as much criticism as possible in order to shift the blame.

The poorly planned advance, the ill-prepared troops, the mistakes of the intelligence service, the fact that many were still wearing summer uniforms as winter arrived, the stretch of supply lines, the difficulty of the terrain, and the total and unexplainable refusal to believe the Chinese were waiting for them, led to a disaster in which thousands of American and United Nations soldiers died, many freezing to death. It was a massive strategic victory pulled off by the communist leader Song Shi-Lun, who won a serious victory over the Allies under the field command of General Oliver P. Smith. The experience was illustrated in the desperate outmaneuvering of advance troops, a high degree of failure of supply and communications, and reasonable military caution that might well be expected by experienced military officers. It is a tale to remind us of the Bataan Death March, or at best the evacuation of Dunkirk.

Yet, through the miracle of propaganda, political denial, selective memory, and historical adjustment, the retreat has become a moment of heroic history.[15] The transformation from reality to myth has been nearly as accepted as Custer's Last Stand. There is no doubt that the men involved displayed as much courage as could possibly be expected, and that hundreds of examples of heroism conducted there should not be forgotten. The facts are, however, that no matter how carefully the lines are drawn, and the picture colored, the People's Volunteer Army, primarily from China, had crossed the Yalu River during the early winter and caught the army and Marines with their pants down. From mid–November until Christmas Eve 1950, they drove the United Nations' forces south until the Allies were evacuated from Hungnam under enemy fire.

While he is not the only one to blame for the decision to move toward the Yalu, the decision reflects a tenacity approaching stubbornness as MacArthur's misinformed decision to allow army and Marine units to cross nearly impassable territory in the middle of the winter, especially when he had no reliable intelligence whatsoever, cannot be explained. It therefore should be investigated far more than the telling of accounts of "bravery in the face of adversity" reflected in numerous memoirs and far too many academic histories.

Questions about the performance of troops and their leaders are still agonizing to contemplate even after so many years, and in most cases the choice has been simply to ignore the question. The number of biographies of significant Korean generals is amazingly small and suggests that few biographers really know how to evaluate them. For the army veterans of the fighting at the Chosin Reservoir, the negative perception of their performance made the wait for official reconsideration long and painful. How has this event become a tactical victory for the Marines and a disgraceful loss for the army that was fighting next to them? Many Marines blame it on an overall army failure.

When we continue to drape this unpleasant reality with flags of patriotism, we fail to add it to the moments in history from which we have great lessons to be learned. Once again, when allowing such myths to dominate our history of the war, we leave unrecorded hundreds of other significant events, and poorly relate the history of hundreds of battles in which we were engaged. Chosin needs to be remembered, not revered. We keep making the same mistakes because we do not learn from those experiences life generates.

The Turks Were Best

The Turks, under the leadership of Brigadier General Tahsin Yazici, arrived in Korea with all the pomp and circumstance of a Marine division. They basked in a blaze of glory and were identified as fierce combat troops despite the fact that they had, in reality, not fought a war since 1923. They arrived with their flowing mustaches, dark mysterious complexion, and the look of fierce aggression in their eyes. Equipped with an exorbitant staff, they dealt with the other nations with an air of independence that made cooperation difficult. War correspondents took one look, decided that these Turks were tough, and reported so before a single encounter. What they were, of course, were pretty ordinary fighting men who, it turned out, were poorly trained, poorly equipped, poorly led, and green to any sort of combat at all.[16]

More than forty-five nations were involved in the Korean War.

These include those who sent troops, offered supplies, provided money, established medical units (neutral as well as military ones), and participated in the cost of the war in one way or another. Most nations that supplied troops ended up suffering wounds and the loss of men killed in action.

The myth was further exaggerated by returning POWs who reported that the Turks had been the least cooperative and most unruly prisoners. A widespread and somewhat exaggerated reputation of the Turks' resistance and toughness as prisons of war was introduced in Stephen Becker's *Dog Tags* (1973) and became a standard against which all other troops are judged.

Accounts of the Turkish units' behavior in battle are varied, but they seemed too often to be the weak point at which a command has extracted, or where a troop of soldiers unexpectedly moved. There was no standard against which to evaluate them, nor was there a consistency of military production that could be considered in the battle plans. The Turks were there and many, especially Ridgway, appreciated them. But the evidence of delivery is still to be located.

A good deal of this is pure fluff and the product of selective thinking and misinformation. Clay Blair, a more careful researcher whose early work is still one of the best, believed that the Turks had created a public image of invaluableness that covered them with glory from the beginning. He is, of course, primarily correct. Some of the early glory began to wear off as the Turks created problems of their own: lack of military discipline, and some long-held resentments between the Turks and the New Zealanders, mortal enemies from World War I. They displayed an unwillingness to cooperate that spilled out into relations with other commands. No communication skills (almost no interpreters available) and an attitude of independence made them difficult. In a significant case, they failed to properly identify the enemy, whereupon they met and destroyed a unit of South Korean regulars.

The best research has been done recently in which the Turks' contribution to the combat success of Eighth army is traced, encounter by encounter, to see if some evaluation of the Turkish effort can be made. Without tools for such an evaluation, the best that can be said is that they performed little better and not much worse than the other nations involved. Certainly they made a contribution, but not necessarily a superior one.

But the stories are told, and retold, and change little with the production of new works. The value of such information as "who was best" is primarily insignificant, other than that perhaps we could learn training methods from them. But this evaluation of troops places the rest of the troops in unreasonable standards of acceptance, and without any additional original research alters the understanding of both troop morale and strategic tactics. The truth is that the Turks underperformed, if they are judged against the standards we have placed on them.[17]

Ike Ended It

"President Eisenhower ended the war," announces a banner at the President's museum and library in Kansas, telling us what we already think we know. Obviously that is not true because the war has not ended. He is, however, generally given credit as being the president when the armistice was finally signed and the combat ended. Limited as our understanding remains, however, the evidence is quite strong that the motivating factor was not President Eisenhower or his strategy that brought about a change in the communist heart, but rather the death of Premier Joseph Stalin. Nevertheless, it was the president's decision to end the fighting without addressing the original cause of the war, and in doing so to leave the seeds of prolonged hostility deeply planted. Many historians and political commentators, like James Edward Smith of the *New York Times*,[18] continue to report on the success of the president's end-of-war endeavors. It is a story much told that President Eisenhower was able to manipulate the situation and bring about a change of heart among the communists that allowed a cease-fire that, while not a victory, was at least an honorable ceasing of hostilities. This is not the whole story by any means.[19]

More significant in the characterization of the president's diplomatic endeavors was the silent agreement made in order to complete the cease-fire. This agreement was nothing less than an act of betrayal to those who had fought the war. The president allowed the armistice to be signed and the fighting stopped by choosing to ignore the fact that American prisoners of war remained in the hands of the communists. Hundreds of Americans, having been taken north into China and even into the Soviet Union, remained unaccounted for. Despite the fact that Operation Little Switch and Operation Big Switch, as well as Operation Glory, were conducted prior to the agreement, the president and his administration knew without a doubt that American prisoners of the communists were still being held. They agreed to the cease-fire nevertheless.

While nothing was said then, and little said since, Senate and House hearings in 1992 and 1996 made it very clear that the president knew that American POWs had been shipped to Russia and China and recognized that their return would be difficult. He decided to let it go—not to push for a release, or even an accounting—for fear that it would delay the agreement and give the communists a chance to rekindle the fighting. The long delay caused by Truman's demand for the repatriation of all prisoners was apparently in vain.[20]

Navy Captain Red McDaniel, six years a prisoner of the communists, summed up the feeling of the veteran when he learned of this decision: "I was prepared to fight, to be wounded, to be captured, and even prepared to die, but I was not prepared to be abandoned."[21] While the administration claims it continued to be concerned about the plight of these men, it apparently was not willing to bring the full force of the United States to bear on their return. It was a calculated risk deemed necessary to accept for fear of further confrontation with China or the Soviet Union.

Official correspondence of the time indicates that the existence of these POWs was well understood. An unknown but apparently substantial number of U.S. military personnel captured in the course of the Korean War are still being held prisoner by communist forces. These individuals will not necessarily be retained in North Korea or in Manchuria, but may be held elsewhere within the Soviet orbit.[22]

Up until his death, Joseph Stalin insisted on taking a hard line at the negotiations. The materials in the Soviet archive do not really tell us why, but Weathersby's suggestion is that the leader may well have thought that, given no expansion of the war, it might be a good thing to keep the United States occupied.

It is often believed that General Eisenhower pushed the communist negotiators into an agreement by rattling the big sword and threatening them with nuclear war. One has to believe that early on in the fighting, atomic warfare was a part of Truman's thinking, and most

70

likely also in Eisenhower's consideration, but by this time it had been ruled out.

It was assumed that President Eisenhower was ready to order the implementation of Operation Shakedown, an all-out offensive that included the potential use of nuclear weapons. The president had made his promised trip to Korea, where General Mark Clark had taken command. The commander had a plan to break the deadlock and move toward victory, but the president never heard Clark's "broad plan for victory." The president, Clark determined, was seeking an honorable truce. The first step, and the one hinted at by official histories, was that he signaled the communists of his intentions through trusted allies. The press seemed to be well informed of the most horrific aspects of NSC 147, and the reaction to this was significant at the time. Scholars will have to wait for a better time until the Soviet, Chinese, and North Korean archives are more easily accessible. But the best bet is still that the death of Stalin sparked a new need for a cease-fire and that the American president responded rather than initiating it.[23]

There is little evidence that such a threat ever reached the ears of the communist leaders. The myth is that the president sent word through India that if the Chinese did not arrive at a cease-fire the president would remove all restraints against nuclear weapons. Neither the threat nor the delivery has ever been documented. Those who knew the president do not believe that he entertained such an idea, nor was it suggested. Rather, historians are more inclined to believe that China's decision to end the war was more related to Joseph Stalin's death and to the larger hope that it would open the way for China to receive more Soviet aid so badly needed to offset Mao's overwhelming expenditure in men and equipment.

Eisenhower had promised during his presidential campaign that he would end the war in Korea and it was very important to him to fulfill that promise even in the face of considerable opposition both from his own administration and the government of the Republic (South) Korea. Secretary of State John Foster Dulles and Secretary of Defense Charles Wilson were against the decision, believing that China needed to be beaten in order to prevent future conflict.

Of course, the misrepresentation of how the armistice came about discounts much of what, if anything, we think we know about it, and admittedly, how we address the other side in this poorly understood cease-fire. Once again the effort to give it the best spin, to defend the status quo, and to provide simple explanations, leads to public confusion and private doubts about the value of the effort.

The sounds of efforts to recover either the POWs or their remains still rumble through the halls of Congress and the White House, but they are rarely accompanied by success. There is every evidence that the United States is simply waiting for them to all go away.[24]

VI

No One Was Invited
to the Parade

The wounded that cannot be salvaged,
are replaced.—*General Mark Willoughby, CSA*

It would be wrong to say that there were no efforts to acknowledge the Korean veterans when they returned. Some did. Families all over the nation anticipated the return of their loved ones and celebrated accordingly. What was lacking was not recognition by Mom and Dad or even from the local Chamber of Commerce, but from the nation. The nation made no effort. What was far worse, the nation felt no obligation to celebrate what had been accomplished. No national uprising of thankfulness. The lack of response, and in some ways the far more devastating feeling that response was a matter of manners and not thanks, has not gone unnoticed. When seen in comparison to the national fervor that accompanied V-E and V-J days, it became quite clear who and what was to be remembered.

The patriotic crowds that greeted much of the troops' return after World War II was missing, but so were the protests and insults of the Vietnam era. Quite frankly, it appears that no one cared enough to protest against Korea. There were very few groundswell movements to challenge either the participation in the event or the expectations of the war. Politically the parties contested wartime events as a part of the routine of doing business, but few if any organized efforts were made either to get America out of Korea, or to evaluate what we were doing there.

Lacking either the passion of a moral crusade or the intensity of an existential crisis, the war was primarily an inconvenience, a nuisance to be dealt with and a relief when it was over. There was business to

73

be finished rather than some national joy to be expressed. Today, so many years later, it is hard to recapture much feeling and there is little to remind us—few sayings, national themes, recognizable activities—to identify what was happening then. There is no "Rosie the Riveter" to remind us of the sacrifice of the Greatest Generation. And for those looking back, either in memory or in efforts to communicate, it was a far different kind of war from those acknowledged today.

Several comments can be made about this difference and how the low-key response, the "get-by" rewards, and the limited benefits all reflected the nation's view of what had happened. But first a look at the difference in war as seen by the Korean generation and that of the Gulf Wars. These are important differences that reflect who was fighting, how they fought, and how it affected them. It is not an evaluation of good or bad, and certainly not a judgment as to difficulty, but simply a comparison.

Not Your Grandson's War

The conflict fought in Korea in 1950–1953 probably had more in common with World War I than it did either the Pacific or European sectors of World War II. This is certainly true of the long stalemate of the final two years. But in any case it was a vastly different war from the "little wars" that followed. Not only did the nature of war change, but the electronic and technical sophistication that followed in the 1960s spread over into the altering nature of life in the military.

In almost every case, today's warrior volunteered for military service and did so for a variety of reasons, not necessarily patriotism. In some very real aspects the military has become a job, a career as much as an obligation. And while there is little doubt about the strong patriotism of those involved in the wars today, there is the realization that they arrive with a different background. Many of those who fought in Korea were recalled (retreads) from World War II, reservists, or those selected by conscription. And while the vast majority of them responded to the country's call out of a strong sense of obligation to the nation, they nevertheless came to the fight with a natural sense of sacrifice, a realization of interrupted lives and delayed progress. This was not a career, this was not a job, this was a demand that they place themselves in harm's way at the request of the American people.[1] For some the return to civilian life, to family and to jobs was once again being put on hold for the sake of the nation. While not a major problem—and little evidence exists of significant numbers who tried to avoid their service—it was at best a delay. For the vast majority of these men and women, they were willingly fulfilling an obligation to the state and they expected their service to be acknowledged.

Look at the concept of casualties. War is no longer fought on the grand scale as it was understood for so long. Of course any death caused by a war is a tragic loss and no less painful because it is one of many. The number of Americans who have died in this century's wars is a matter of considerable regret. But in terms of numbers, war today is no longer as costly as it has been, at least to the participants. At the battle of Monte Cassino in 1944, more than 185,000 men died, five times as many as died in the Korean War. More Americans were killed in one day at the battle of Pork Chop Hill than were killed in the entire Gulf War, Somalia, and Bosnia-Herzegovina combined. In our current war, the names of those killed in action are broadcast, and often those watching the evening news can see the arrival of the body, whereas it is still hard to locate an accurate list of the names of those killed in the Korean War. If nothing else, the concept of acceptable casualties has changed, and as a nation we are far more conscious of the single life than we once were.

In looking back on those years of service, many a young man is aware of the paradox of his memories; he was never alone and yet he was always isolated. There was always someone there, often only a few feet from the rows of bunks they shared, but there was little of the attachment many might have expected. From the first entry-physical to the departure gates at Fort Sheridan, the gathering youth were in a crowd, often standing in a long line. But other than being in the army, they were not well attached to the service; they had no particular home. For the Korean soldier, each moment, from getting on the bus heading for basic training to the final discharge, was accomplished alone, as an individual, not as part of a unit or a command, not as a part of something to which he belonged. Coming and going, the Repo Depot was home, the neighbors as migrant as themselves, and the role as replaceable parts for an active unit was well understood. In the course of service, the individual was subject to isolated command, moved at will, unassociated with anything permanent. There were no home-town units, no regiments made up of friends, for assignments were much like the popular "just on time delivery" later made famous by the Japanese. When these men returned home, there were very few "reunions," as few felt any particular attachment to a unit, or saw any advantage in gathering with them once again. Despite all the talk about brotherhood and comrades, there was a lot of togetherness but few lasting relations.

There is also another kind of isolation involved: that is the separation from the world from which they came. Today's warrior has every opportunity to maintain contact with his individual worlds, through phone calls home, e-mails, face-to face-contact via smart phones, among other things. Even while separated by miles and by danger, the individual soldiers are able to maintain connections, to be a part of things, to be remembered. The fact that those involved can and do remain in contact with their home base changes the emotional tone of their participation.

From the perspective of sixty years and the long separation most Korean veterans experienced, it is hard to say if that situation is better or worse: which is the hardest on the GI. The soldier on the line, no matter where he was, needed two things: his rifle and the postman. In almost every case the occasional letter was the only connection with the world he had left behind. Time, distance, terrain, weather, all worked against the GI, and the letter, if it came at all, often arrived a month after having been mailed. The young warrior of today is literally able to call home after a long patrol and check out things going on there, to watch a child's birth on smart phone, to take classes from an online university, to maintain relationships on Facebook, to be reminded of someone's love. Aware that communication delivers bad news and tension as well as good news and support, the anxiety of not knowing what is going on at home has nevertheless been cut considerably. Picture phones provide moments of a child's growth, texting provides participation in major decision making, and the like. The warrior of today avoids much of the sense of isolation that was the hallmark of Korean service.

The same is true, of course, in terms of the delivery of "home" to those at war. No one during the Korean War would have expected to see broadcasts of the World Series, and the only football scores that were recounted were the Army/Navy game. The occasional rear-guard troop at division rear might see a one-reel film of *I Love Lucy* or even a rare movie, but it was rare indeed. The USO performers were great breaks in service, but these units did not often make it to the front lines.

In acknowledging the difference in the fighting of the Korean War and the later post–Vietnam role, one must take into consideration the impact of duration in the life of the grunt fighting on the ground. Consider the day-after-day extension of each and every condition. Consider a sleeping bag covered with snow, not one night or two but weeks on end. Or eating nearly cold food from a can or a long line at the field kitchen. In most respects the living conditions of those who participate in today's wars are vastly more civilized than those endured by soldiers who slugged it out twenty-four hours a day, seven days a week, in the heat, or the mud, or the snow, or the rain.

While there is no doubt that the killing conditions are as bad today as anytime or anywhere, it is nevertheless true that today's service personnel and combat warrior returns from his assignment to reasonable housing, beds, showers and even air conditioning. They are well fed and clothed, well equipped, and maintained in conditions as normal as possible. And, even more unusual, they are in areas where they can regroup in reasonable safety. They even have mess halls and never-ending supplies of coffee. If this is not better than what was experienced by the GI who fought in Korea, it is at least different from what was experienced, and thus remembered as war, by those who fought against the North Koreans and Chinese in the frozen expanses of Korea.

There is as well the question of comradeship. The Korean War veteran, like all veterans, will recall strong friendships, bonding of a moment in which the presence of another made a significant difference in how he survived. Most call this comradeship and take it very seriously. And there is no intention here to suggest anything that would lessen that experience or weaken what ties remain. But it is not the same.

As it is explained by so many authors, comradeship appears to be the closest thing to a utopian state of being that most people experience, and there is much to be said about its enduring power. These moments of comradeship, even short-lived, are very important. And while it was most likely not as common in the mobile nature of the army of 1950 as it was in World War II, it was nevertheless remembered.

While the differences between wartime buddies and home front receptors is obvious, what is not so obvious is that veterans returning were looking for much the same sort of relationship with those who had fought the same war, but this time from home.

The home front acceptance of the war effort is significantly different. If in nothing else, in some small way this collective acceptance of responsibility helps the veterans to transfer some of the psychological burdens of wartime service to society. Such gratitude will not eradicate combat stress, nor address every veteran's experience, but it would have expanded the base of those carrying the load of accountability. In this case America did not really ever go to war.

The country was different. For the first time the American people did not appear to have the passionate involvement that had been the case in previous years. Some historians suggest this was the result of President Truman's belief that the nation could avoid hardship while fighting a war, and that the people should not have to suffer the hardships experienced during World War II. Melinda Pash, in her excellent book *In the Shadow of the Greatest Generation*, suggests that the American people never really gave the war much thought in the first place. Certainly the apathetic attitude of the home front had much to do with the lack of interest shown to the returning veteran. "No one seemed interested in hearing about my adventure, so I just stopped talking," the tough old veteran told an interviewer. "I just stopped talking."[2]

Nothing had been done to prepare the home front for the return of the veteran. Few even knew they were coming.

Recognition

If, as is being suggested, sadness reflects the attitude of the Korean veteran, then silence reflects their behavior. While few veterans who were involved in the traumatic fighting talked about that aspect of it, the Korean veteran has been silent even about his service. World War II veterans, and especially Vietnam veterans spoke openly about the noncombat aspects of their involvement, made an effort to identify themselves as veterans, and organized reunions. They waved what used to be called "the bloody shirt."[3] The Korean veterans did not; they were primarily invisible. There was generally little announcement of their service. It is not that they were ashamed, for they were not; they just did not feel it necessary to so identify themselves. They put their medals in the drawer, hung up their flying or tanker jackets, shed their old unit cap, and let the war slide. You very rarely saw a Korean veteran wearing the odds and ends of his old uniforms, or displaying patches or unit emblems. For half a century there were no license plates announcing "I am a Korean War Veteran."

General Ridgway, who led the return to Seoul after the Chosin retreat, was criticized in Congress for the names he selected for his operations, such as Operation Killer, Operation Strangle. His reply was typically Ridgway: "I am not by nature open to selling war to people as an only mildly unpleasant business that required very little in the name of blood." He went on to suggest that Congress should not be afraid to talk about what they are not afraid to ask others to do.[4]

Some who serve in the veterans' hospitals report differences when working with Korean veterans. This point of view may only reflect those coming for aid, but still presents an interesting picture. "They often appear cautious," one young nurse suggested. "When coming for aid they appear reluctant almost hesitant to ask, not always sure what to do next. Also not sure if they qualify as veterans. They are always polite, on many occasions timid, as if asking for something that is not their due."[5]

In the main, these men are not interested in being pointed out or noticed. They have the tendency to listen carefully to what is being said about their war, but rarely would interrupt or correct. One physical therapist who dealt with veterans from a series of wars suggested it was as if the Korean soldier had returned to the military to receive new orders.

Part of this calm seems to be related to a wait-and-see attitude; the reoccurring phrases "whatever" and "the way the ball bounces" reflected a sort of patience akin to fatalism. An almost robot-like distance that passes for lack of interest. A lack of connection that can be traced to the inability to find closure to the war itself. This realization that the battle they fought is not decided and, if it ever is, it will be decided sometime in the future and some distance from the bloody fields. This lack of interest seems to contrast with the assertive individualism of the soldiers of World War II and Vietnam.[6]

These realities of acceptance, or lack of it, certainly do not qualify as causes for PTSS. It is not the same as the traumatic experience on the field of battle. But whatever it is, it has accompanied many Korean veterans all their lives and the isolation of their service seemed to be accentuated by the accumulation of poor responses, unfulfilled expectations, separations, and suspicions. Little research has been done on this aspect of the war, and much that has been done is primarily speculation. But perhaps the accumulated insults delivered over the years may have something to say about it.

"More and more," reported Staff Sergeant Wayne Holmes, "I feel like a piece of furniture in the room, and have learned that silence is my best form of social response." He had found some safety, perhaps even isolation, in his own silence. "To whom do you talk when no one else seems to know the words," he asked.

The army took somewhere between eight and sixteen weeks to train most men to be soldiers, to unbind them from the hampering restrictions of humanity, to make them obedient, and to provide them discipline. It took less than six hours to muster out and release these same men to civilian life. It was not enough time.

The anger was still there, and while tempered considerably by being out of harm's way, it often rose up in these men for reasons that were totally irrational even for a primarily rational man. The government had spent millions of dollars making hard and unrepentant men who had learned a lesson they could not easily forget: violence works. The departing wisdom was short and well-meaning; "Use toilet paper, don't say fuck around your parents, don't call everyone sir." All this along with a five-minute film shown in a halfhearted attempt to remind the soldier of the implied chastity of American women. And remember: American gooks are our friends.

Most of these men had answered when called and served when selected, and they did so with little thought of doing anything else. If asked, and few were, why they were there, most would have said something about duty or patriotism. While there was certainly a large amount of talk, most of it was grumbling hidden as conversation. These men and women, whose war was sandwiched between the good war to save the world and the bad war of imperialism, were a generation in their own right. They were identified by what they shared, the uncommon effects of the Great Depression, a war of unprecedented expansion and violence, and a still-maintained sense of duty and obligation to their nation. Theirs had been an experience of shared unity, of coming together for a common cause; victory was the nation's goal. It was perhaps the last generation to be characterized by a sense of unquestioned obedience and trust.

They appeared to be anxious to march to the same drummers that had accompanied their fathers and brothers, husbands and sweethearts, off to the great crusade. Interestingly, it has become evident that a significant number of Korean veterans did not tell their wives or children that they had been in Korea. Of the populations that visit the Center for the Study of the Korean War over a year's time, much of it is made up of older women and teenage children who, on their husbands' and fathers' deaths, had just learned they served in Korea. Why would this be true?

A familiar phrase was that "the sons of the well-to-do go to college and the sons of the rest go to Korea." But this is not as much true as it was believed. The likelihood of military service was impacted by a lot of things from marital status to reserve obligation, and in the main it was only the sons of farmers who could be assured of beating the draft. Once Congress had passed the Selective Service Act of 1948 with its Universal Military Training bill, young men who came into maturity during and after World War II found the draft an ever-present force in their lives.

What with a lower draft age, the average age of the Korean War soldier was only twenty-three. That is two years older than the age of the World War I American, and three years older than those in World War II. Contrary to the popular opinion that women were anxious to serve in the Armed Services, volunteers did not keep up with demand, and widespread campaigns were conducted to see if women could be induced to join up. Many men or women who did so seem to reflect the attitude of this one young male volunteer: "My intention was to kill a few North Koreans or Chinese, maybe get a small wound, and be taken care of by a June Allyson or Doris Day type nurse."[7]

At the same time, most acknowledged the frail bargain they had made with themselves that allowed them to focus their minds and most of their emotions on survival. While few knew why or how it was happening, they were nevertheless aware that they were changing. Yet it is hard to explain what they were feeling because the language they had available failed them. The civilian-issued adjectives, nouns, verbs

81

and adverbs all seemed to be developed for communication in a totally different world. The unsaid stacked up and accumulated as feelings of isolation and lack of appreciation continued. When the going-home moment arrived, they knew it was over, and yet they also knew that it was never going to be over. Home did not appear to be the calm and peaceful place so long anticipated and envisioned.

For some returning, it appeared they were sneaking back into the Unites States, arriving at deserted docks away from the crowd busy with other lives. To the thousands looking down at the nearly vacant wharves, there was the feeling of dislocation. Coming home should have meant something. The reactions were mixed; no bands played, it appeared darker than when the ship had left Korea, and the dogs of the K-9 Corps were the first off the ship.

The men aboard ship played cards, performed KP, drilled, and engaged in long, dull conversations about nothing. Where was the comradeship? These were casual acquaintances brought on by their geographical proximity. Where was the kind of comradeship portrayed in films like *Band of Brothers*, and yet totally lacking in Korean War films like *Steel Helmet* and *Pork Chop Hill*? Membership in the brotherhood of arms is hard to maintain when you have been a replacement puppet, rather than a part of the body politic. In World War II, for example, men were often drafted together, trained together, spent two to four years in the same outfit, and fought, played, and survived together. They even rotated together, often to an approximate geographical spot. Among these men some fantastic friendships developed. But looking about the great rusty ship heading home from Korea, how many men looked out and saw anyone they knew?

The primary composition of the fighting force was small squads and outposts, manned by small groups from vastly different nations, as well as races and religions. The groups were far more likely to argue than to bond. A lot of promises of long-term friendship were made, but the reality is few of them were ever followed up. Most Korean veterans will tell you that "what happened in Korea stays in Korea," including many relationships. It could be the nature of that war, or the character of those called on to fight it, or perhaps a total misreading of the information, but there is a good bit of evidence to suggest that few Korean veterans made deep and lasting friendships that carried on after the war.[8]

Such relations that were formed were solid and provided both physical and psychological support to those involved. But something about them, some small part of their character, is noticeable. Few carried on beyond the end of the war.[9] Some, not sharing a common home town, let geography eat away at their connection. Some discovered they did not want reminders of previous events and allowed the friendship to fade along with other memories. Many remained quiet about such relationships.

Home was a massive enclosure in which they reconstructed the GI. Marching into the sea side of a large warehouse, they moved like meat through a processing plant. Men chatted about what was on their mind. "Hell, I was scared when I was in Korea," reported Wayne Funmaker, a Sioux Indian who was standing naked in front of a table on which was a sign that read "Directions." He had served with the 31st Field Artillery. "I am more scared now. What if I don't recognize my wife?"

Being a civilian is not like riding a bicycle; you don't just do it again naturally. Lewis Oglethorpe, who had started to write his memoirs but found it too difficult, voiced the feeling in part: "I would be hard put to suggest the differences in me but while I felt strong and confident I was totally unprepared for any of the responsibility that my new status gave me." He went on to speak of the sense of finality the service offered him: "My assumed personality hung like a cloud over me. I had lost my innocence. Whatever trust I established was gone, whatever beliefs I had in the goodness of man (or woman) were weakened to the point of breaking, whatever hope I had for mankind or what my folks used to call salvation was a lost cause indeed. Indeed I was excited about coming home but I did not have a lot of expectations for my world."[10]

In time, as they returned, they discovered that the nation had moved on without waiting for them; it had outpaced them and provided little evidence they were welcome to return. So they felt forgotten. Poised uncomfortably between the heroic victors of the Second World War and the angry voices of Vietnam, these quiet soldiers had fought an ambiguous conflict with an ambiguous ending. It was a time when ambiguity was avoided even more harshly than today.

This veteran of which we speak so commonly: who was he or even she? They are a part of an elite group who, in the course of the fighting, are estimated to have numbered at about one point eight million Americans. They included older men who had served in World War II, reservists who were called up, some volunteers, and draftees, men who were drawn from national conscription. Few wanted to go but very few indeed objected; the response was fairly automatic for this generation. The youngest who served are now entering their 80s or 90s and are passing away at the average rate of a thousand a day. During the fighting, more than 34,000 died and another 103,000 were wounded, some as many as five times. Nearly 8,000 are still missing in action. If a commonality can be found, it is this: there is an anonymity to the people who fought it. And they were no more aware or equipped to remember it than was the society into which they were returning.

VII

The Shock of No Gun Ri

Man stands in his own shadow,
and wonders why it is so dark. —*Zen Proverb*

When the first reports of the massacre at No Gun Ri began to filter into the civilian population, a great uproar resulted. The charge was that American soldiers, defending the line near a small bridge at No Gun Ri, fired on and killed a large number of Korean civilians crossing the bridge ahead of the fighting. The soldiers, who were retreating, were being pressured by Communist troops. Newspapers sensationalized the event and used it to identify other suspected atrocities and to bolster against the evils of war. Calls for investigations, demands for heads to roll, and insistence that policies be established swept the bewildered public. That, of course, is what is so shocking. Not that innocent civilians would be killed in a war, but that the American people would know so little about the wars they sent their children to fight.

Pray tell, what did they think war was, that they would be so astounded by the war crimes it generated? Of course, civilians are often killed, raped, and even murdered, villages unnecessarily destroyed, enemy personnel mistreated, just as there were unaccountable heroics, humanitarianisms, soldiers who took in the orphans, fed the villagers, and provided medical aid. What does the nation think is going to happen when they train our angry young men to go and kill their angry young men? How can we be so disconnected, so lacking in understanding, and yet so quick to unleash war after war? It is ignorance, nothing more. Our adjustment has been far too easy. It's an unfortunate human trait that we can take the most awful realities and adjust them to become the acceptable and the commonplace. The death of one man, Stalin is (falsely) supposed to have said, is a tragedy, while the death of a million is a statistic. This tendency, at least, as a description of the human response, is overwhelming.

In acknowledging the discomfort displayed in the announcement of this event, it became obvious that the average American citizen has no concept of what war is like, how it is fought, and the cost in humanitarian characteristics weakened among its human participants. It is obvious as well that they have no concept of the increasing mingling of civilian and military factors that are taking place in combat, and the degree to which the idea of nonparticipant is more a myth than a reality.

A substantial source of this ignorance is that no one talks about war. Not just casual conversation about the "state of the war," but in-depth conversations about what war consists of, why they are fought, and maybe even why men are willing to fight them. When the young man sweated it out as a replacement at Camp Stoneman, he was usually in his late teens or early twenties and had no idea what he was involved in. He did not know what to expect. But far more important, he did not know what was expected of him. No one had ever talked to him about war.

In this country it is fairly easy to get through twelve years of public education without ever being exposed either to history or historical thought. Under the influence of publicly accepted social sciences, ethnic studies, sensitive history and runaway reductionism, educators seek to assume some understanding of the total picture from the dissection of the parts. As educational theory emerges and facilities expand, the nature of the curriculum is weakened by the injection of something called "social science" into what had once been historical awareness. In twelve years of education, many a young person will never have been talked to about war.[1]

As it is easier and easier to identify the lack of such education in the secular community, one might wonder why the vacuum has not been filled, or at least addressed, by those responsible for moralistic justification. The religious community, weakened but still powerful, has taken no responsibility for teaching its members about war. After all, church is where you learn about values and meaning. But through the long sessions of Sunday School, hours of off-key singing, and boring sermons, one can hear the word "peace" many times, but no one is there to explain about war. While the churches have a long and unfortunate history of supporting wars, and maintains its metaphoric association with the "armies of the Lord," they have done very little indeed to address the many beliefs that cause wars.

A good many of those young men who served in Korea learned most of what they knew about war from the movies. Hundreds of well-scripted movies were available to direct public thinking. Many from that generation can, to this day, recall some of these movies and what feelings they identified with. At such an age, death, especially death presented as glorified and patriotic, had little fear. There is little said about the brokenness that is often involved. A brokenness that threatens to capitulate to what John Eldridge, in the religious context, calls "the traitor within." Known to many men and women, it is the fear under stress they would be inclined to run, or even to surrender to the enemy. We are, as FDR warned us, afraid of fear. Afraid that the strength of our resolve has the potential of being betrayed by the fear that lies hidden and unannounced within us. It is the awareness of this fear, rather than the fear itself, that eats at men and women and calls them to find the answer. In some often undisclosed manner they seek the fight in which to prove that they would not be afraid. That they are indeed willing to give it all for God, for country, for friends in need. That when the time comes they stand alone and generally unprepared to challenge their moments of destiny, they will nevertheless prevail.

Certainly one source of knowledge about war would be the discipline of history, especially military history. While the popular reading of military history seems to be holding its own, even growing in some areas, the study of military history is less and less available than it was a decade or so ago. Military history, when taught in the academies, tends to focus on the how rather than the why, and even military historians who write on more specific aspects of the war rarely are telling us about war. They are telling us about historical events.

It seems strange that at a time when the United States is involved in two or three wars, when the interest in the publication of books on military history is increasing, when Hollywood is rediscovering the military films of World War II, and when classes on military history draw students when offered, that colleges and universities all over the country are closing down their military history departments. Even those that still provide some instruction in military history have diminished in size, many with only one staff member. As it is now, few colleges or universities in the United States have a trained military historian on the staff. The exceptions are in the military academies, which generally tell us more about how to go to war than they do why.

The same phenomenon is recognized in other places as well. The prime journal of the discipline, the *American Historical Review*, rarely carries an article on military history—that is, on war—believing that there are other, far more significant topics for consideration. Many academics have the notion that military historians are, as a breed, right-wing, morally suspect, and in most cases just plain obsessed. What we need, it is suggested, is more on the "left out" history. The emergence of gender consciousness, labor studies, racial and ethnic considerations, economic history, urban history, and a whole range of "specialists" have left little time and less money for consideration of the military. It is hard to offer an explanation for those who seemed determined to ignore the military aspect of our national culture. Surely they are missing something. Most importantly, they fail to understand that it is essential to a democratic populace that its citizens have some knowledge about the nature of the wars that they send their young people to fight. With an all-volunteer army, the majority of the citizens have no contact with the concept of the military; they do not even know anyone who is or has been in the military.

More significant is to try to tell the story of one's life and not mention those moments of violence, the fights, the muggings, the rapes, the assessments of victory and defeat, for that is to leave the story untold. And in such a state, one is likely to make poor decisions based on false assumptions. We continue to make poor military decisions because the average American's understanding of organized violence is minuscule.[2]

If we are not going to teach military history in our educational system, then it may well be time to reinstate the draft, to reenact a selective service agency that organizes conscription and the reintroduction of the citizen soldier. There are a lot of good reasons for reconsidering this. One is to acknowledge that some of the misinformation we have to deal with comes from the gap that currently separates the average American from the military. The situation is not only unwise, it is dangerous. When most people think of the military, they consider it a vast military complex, but fail to realize that fewer than 2 percent of our population is involved. It should give pause. As a nation we honor the military, in some cases we fear it, but we most certainly do not understand it. It is proper to say that we love our troops, but with all due respect, we would much rather not be bothered to think about them too much. It is better to let them focus on themselves. As time passes and we are willing to live with an all-volunteer military, the percentage of persons who have served in the military gets smaller and smaller, and they appear to be coming from a less diverse group of persons.

Service in the military, like in early Germany and the Old South, is moving more toward becoming a family tradition, and in so doing is at odds with our traditional view of how a democracy spreads the burden. While there is much to be said practically and traditionally for our current system, there is also a strong argument for universal military training. As in Israel, everyone would need to serve. A nation in which all have some acknowledgment of the military, some feel for the emotions of war, and the realization that peacekeeping is the burden of defense, is well informed. In the United States, at the moment, the military is for most people an exotic territory.

One of the blowbacks of a civilian armed forces is that enough comfort with the military would allow us to find humor in the situation and, more important, the freedom to question their role and competence as we would any other institution. As James Fallows so carefully pointed out, there is little humor about the military these days. There used to be. In the years following World War II, when so many were familiar with the military, they were willing to make fun of it. Even *M*A*S*H*, which presented a satirical attitude about the competence of the military, could present a fierce disagreement about Vietnam (though it was set in Korea). But these days you see very little of this sort of humor, and thus the subtle criticism it provides.

The danger of a volunteer militia lies not only in the independence of the military, but the lack of knowledge among the constituents. Since service is not required, we are generally represented by, and taken into war by, men and women who have not served. The decisions for war are made by leaders who do not know the language, have never felt the emotions of combat, and do not understand anything of the long-term human costs that follow such an involvement. As a people we have decided to compartmentalize war, sealing it off from the rest of our lives. We know nothing of war, make no effort to know about war, and then are astonished by what happens in wartime.

We neither want nor need a massive military made up of draftees from all over America. But without some form of conscription, we will never bridge the civilian-military divide that has grown during the four decades of an all-volunteer armed services. It simply isn't realistic to expect every American to be involved even in wartime. But in view of the consequences, it seems perfectly reasonable for each citizens to have some personal experience with the military, and thus some basis to establish an informed opinion.

The War Lovers

Peace organizations have not been all that successful in modern times. Even the best of them expound an aggressiveness to their position that creates for many a serious concern about their final intent. A far more significant criticism of their overall efforts is the degree to which they avoid the fact that some men and women love war. They love war and what war is. And, in all honesty, these persons are not particularly interested in bringing about an end to war. The quote attributed to General George Patton, in the movie about his life, says it all: "God help me, I do love it so." War is a powerful attraction, a paradox that lures men into battle even as it frightens them nearly to death.

Why is it that so many love something that seems to be unlovable? Many are inclined to close their minds to history and substitute some animal instinct in man, like the need to hunt found in the tiger, that makes him go to war. But that may be far too simple an accounting. War is a highly worked out plan for theft. It started when the first group of men managed to create an abundance and others wanted it. That is where war comes from, that is its beginning, but why do men love it so? Is it simply the fulfillment of greed?

Dozens of books and hundreds of articles have been written trying to explain why men go to war, and many of them conclude, in some fashion or the other, that men go to war simply because they love it. While few men who have been involved in war would want to talk about it, it seems obvious there is some aspect about it that they appreciated and miss. Among them, and deeply ingrained, is that it provides a prolonged intensity like nothing else, other perhaps than sex. This is not a romanticized love as found in stories of King Richard, it is not a deep-seated psychological desire to kill as might be the case with a psychopath, but rather a love that cannot be explained in the language available to civilians. It is, if you will, the lust of the eye, the "I can't believe this shit!" experience. This participation in the massive passion for extremes that last for hours on end.

It is that moment when everything common becomes uncommon, everything routine loses its routine, when boredom and apathy, dullness and sameness, are swept away in a moment of incredible excitement. This is the gift of war: the promise of intensification of all things simple. This C-ration may be the last rations and thus it is the best, this sunrise just before battle is the best sunrise, this kiss is the last kiss and thus the best kiss of all kisses.

In all of history it seems that we are aware that governments do a poor job of avoiding war, but we have never figured out why individuals seem to find war so acceptable, even exhilarating. Perhaps it is enough to say that combat satisfies some sort of human need. The limited ability to explain it might be found in the conflict that resides in most of us, between our desire to be special, unique, and individual while at the same time to be a member of the group, a citizen of the tribe. Only two institutions in history have addressed this need. One is the organized confusion of institutional religion, and the second is war. In religion the Way of the One and the Way of the Many become rehearsed in the paradoxical, yet faith promoted acceptance of a man who can be God and a society in which one gains admittance by the giving of oneself. In war men find the individualizing growth of expanded experience, heightened perception, and a magnified awareness of the self, even while such experience makes one more involved as a part of the tribe.

Only the religious conviction or the war experience can deliver what they promised by providing a temporary experience for solving the conflict within us. Post Traumatic Stress Syndrome (Disorder) may not be a totally dreadful experience of recalling a terrible event; it might also be a part of returning to a world in which there are no ways to work through the crisis of the one and the many. Returning means that you will never experience either the adrenalin of such experience or the boldness of such intimacy.

There are many men and women who see in the provisions of war the opportunity to test themselves in the chaos of battle. To find out what is the merit of their soul. Some, like Theodore Roosevelt, perhaps saw it as a much-needed opportunity to test his manhood on the field of battle. Whatever the reason, this "terrible addiction and wretched curse" has followed man all through time. Some find it too tempting as a place to test their manhood, and many an old man who regrets he did not do so tries to compensate. They do not see the horror, the banality, the fear, the tedium, the pettiness. That is why it is such a dangerous temptation.

VIII

The Infidelity
of the Storytellers

Tell me the facts and I'll learn,
Tell me the truth and I'll believe.
but tell me a story and it will be in my heart forever.
—*Native American Proverb*

Storytelling is the oldest form of narrative communication known to mankind. As far as we know, it has been around as long as human beings were able to grunt out some simple narrative. Stories teach history, report events, settle arguments, make sense of things, help us remember, celebrate and formulate explanations, as well as pass on wisdom, convince, exchange moral values, invent and encourage metaphysical experience, and of course, entertain. Basically the story event consists of the story itself (the plot), the storyteller, and the listener (reader), and while all are important to the success of the event, it is the storyteller who is the most significant as well as being the most volatile.

The success of Garrison Keillor is an example of the fact that many people still love a good story and will listen to one even when they are immune to everything else. Once a person has started to listen to a story, it is difficult to pull away. It is true, however, that the growth in technology and the expansion of demography has made the story more and more formal, cut down on the individualized nature of the craft, and both consolidated the story and spread it more quickly. Like religion and the dance that were first, and perhaps best, celebrated on the street, storytelling has moved indoors and has taken on the characteristic of the theater. And in so doing, it has changed to the point that stories become stylized and have assumed a truth and a falsity in their own right.

For modern men and women the venue has altered, and that which was once maintained by the storyteller has increasingly become the role of the historian, the news media, the filmmaker, and the entertainment business. The desire to hear the story pervades those aspects of society that provide them, and so they become increasingly effected by what they want to hear. The storyteller and the plot give way to the wishes of the reader. And while it is the story that we stopped to hear, it is the storyteller who has unwittingly taken on the responsibility of preserving the past, of reporting the present, of anticipating the future. It is the modern storyteller—the newscaster, the movie producer, the historian, the novelist and the musician—upon whom the responsibility now lies.

In the case of the Korean War, there is reason to believe that these modern tellers of the tale have not done very well. They have not preserved the story as honestly as the American people deserve. They have been too much influenced by the increasing poverty of the reader. The media's reporting lacked both interest and integrity; the historian has damaged the story with his analysis and lack of comprehension. The filmmaker has not only reverted to the search for markets at the expense of the story, but has also misrepresented the event and violated its participants in the name of "poetic license." The novelist and the musician and the artist have not used their craft to record this significant event in any manner that speaks to the people.

Consider as well the scope of the stories that have not been told. Stories of the war that reflect its culture far more than the invasion at Inchon or President Eisenhower's visit to the war zone. Stories which have as much to tell us about war, and about this war, as political analysis. Stories that are now hinted at, but the details of which are still hidden in the shadows of misinformation. Think of the impact of such stories as the Tiger Death March, which, like the Bataan march, killed large numbers of American soldiers, but which was primarily unreported.[1] Or perhaps Operation Chicken Stealer or Cat and Mouse, or perhaps some comment about the Prisoner of War Olympic Games played out with United Nations prisoners of war, who competed against each other in an Olympic style track meet sponsored by the communists.

Or perhaps the government, or at least the investigative arm of the large press corps, might well have informed the American people that more than 70,000 Russians—including pilots, ground crews, anti-aircraft gunners, and engineers—were involved in the war, taking the lives of the citizens of the conflicting nations. The Russian MiG pilots tried to talk only in Chinese, flew against our jets, and shot down our bombers. So afraid were the Russians that the United Nations might steal secrets from the improved MiG that they forbade their pilots from flying over South Korea or the sea where a downed plane might be salvaged.

Neither government made this known to their own people for fear that if known the people would rise up in both nations to demand either more retaliation or increased involvement. How could such a story have been kept quiet and even denied twenty and thirty years later[2] if the press had done their job, or the historians broadened their fields of inquiry, or the novelist drawn our attention?

It is not the purpose here to lay blame on anyone or any institution, but rather to react to how the storyteller has affected, and continues to affect, the manner in which the war is remembered and the degree to which it is forgotten.

The Press

From the wide acceptance of such "classic works" as T.R. Fehrenbach's *This Kind of War: The Classic Korean War History*[3] or Marguerite "Maggie" Higgins's *The War in Korea*, early reports of the events in Korea included imaginatively created information that the reporter was in no position to know.[4] And as the war continued, the press maintained a strange silence about some things that the public had every right to know. Such "game changers" became a part of the management of the news. That is information that was so orchestrated to produce smooth background music for the folks back home. Just as silent was the press's comments about the heavy involvement of troops and equipment of the Japanese, a neutral nation under occupation by the United Nations and forbidden to go to war. Vague and misleading were communications concerning the Allied decision to cross over the 38th Parallel and head north, an action that was in direct violation of the very UN resolution that originally authorized the involvement.

The first account of the war in American newspapers was on 25

June 1950 when the *New York Times* and the *Boston Daily Globe* published reports of the invasion. Early accounts focused on the surprise of the invasion, the immediate losses, and the evacuation of Americans. From the beginning, aware of the danger that their reporting might be of aid to the enemy, the press corps imposed a voluntary censorship restricting their comments to more generalized statements. Very few correspondents were available in the area, and those who were had little experience. The accounts were more opinion and commentary than they were reporting. Maggie Higgins, a colorful character who became news in her own right, wrote of the most appalling military disorganization she had ever seen.[5]

The sensational coverage, however limited in quantity, quickly lessened, and the media response as the war dragged on appears irresponsible. But there are some explanations for what happened, even if few excuses. To begin with, the original and investigative nature of the reporting was greatly stymied by a combination of self-imposed censorship, hardships, military management, and the desire for human comfort.

From the very beginning the dispatching of stories from Korea presented problems of their own. The logistical challenge facing the correspondents made reporting difficult and the lack of delivery systems made them dependent on the military. The limited infrastructure of the poor nation increased the difficulty, making it nearly impossible to get information back to their papers, even when collected. The correspondent became more and more dependent on the military for the use of their limited facilities. There were no established news agencies in Korea and those that might have been available were quickly lost. Air flights in and out of the nation had far more necessary things to carry than dispatches and films for the folks back home.

The harshness of the countryside and the mounting pressure of advancing enemy troops made movement about Korea, the coverage of battles or the reporting on a single command, costly. The difficulty of terrain and the poor roads and communication networks meant that the correspondent had the most difficulty when embedded with the troops themselves. The old role models established by Ernie Pyle in World War II were hard to emulate. The efforts were not without cost. Eleven war correspondents were killed during the Korean War as some made the effort to address their responsibilities despite the danger.[6]

96

The war, particularly at the beginning, moved quickly, and when a reporter wanted a story it was necessary to get military support for travel, and logistics while at the front. They were hampered as well by the inability to establish safe zones from which they could operate.

The correspondents in Korea did not seem to share the same sense of commitment that had been witnessed in World War II. One observer suggested they appeared to be more reporters than correspondents, meaning that they simply passed on what was given to them. They carried, as a backdrop, a lack of appreciation for the enemy forces, but also for the South Korean people and the ROKA. Edward R. Murrow, reporting by radio, informed the public that "Korea was a flea bitten nation where devastating American firepower had left dead villages scattered throughout the countryside."[7] In general the press was hard on the primitive Koreans and mostly uncritical of American behavior in which defeats were unrecognized and setbacks underplayed. As the war continued, the coverage lessened and at some points nearly faded away, replaced in part by the Cold War and the decision by the press that one encompassed the other.

Living in the shadow of the Red Scare, people were frightened by what was happening, and saw malicious interests in the communist aggressors. There was only a small and vastly concerned audience for any dissenting opinions or critical analysis at this time. At home, senior officials of the government took exception to some of the more critical comments by such persons as Eleanor Roosevelt, who pushed the government to tone down reports that put Americans in a poor light and depressed morale. Consideration and coverage eventually reflected the belief of the Truman Administration that the real danger remained in Europe, not Asia, and especially not Korea. The press seemed unable to draw its attention away from the idea that Korea was taking its directions from Moscow.

A key to understanding the nature of the coverage, however, can be linked to the press's increasing dependence on the military for war news. Because of this, during the war official information, even of questionable validity, was frequently accepted by the press unchallenged.

The presence of self-imposed censorship gave way to military censorship in December of 1950.[8] The correspondents became more and more dependent on a "pooling" system in which the military would provide a briefing session and the information would be shared among the correspondents. The result, obviously, was both a lack of individual insights and the filtering of the content; the same stories often appeared in many papers at the same time, using the same words.

The *Washington Post* responded to the end of the Korean War with a matter-of-fact article presented without jubilation or honor; it was a peace without victory.[9] Much of the print media responded as if waiting for the other shoe to drop. It was almost as if they were unsure of the source of their information or unwilling to extend themselves too far for fear of being proven wrong.

Radio

Just about everyone in America had a radio, and listening to the radio was a nightly adventure for many people. It was the source of family entertainment, especially among rural communities. It was on the radio that Americans got the first word of the attacks on Pearl Harbor and news of VE and VJ Days. And while most saw it as entertainment, they did rely on it to some degree for news. The news accounts were generally brief and cryptic. Nevertheless, the radio is where people got much of the war coverage, and they continued to do so during the events in Korea. Transcripts from this era show that most of the news was "read," that is, presented as if the announcer were reading from the newspaper, and so there was little if any comment about events. The news, usually available at 1700 and 2200 hours, was primarily announced. Edward R. Murrow, who had already established himself as the "newsman" from his commentary from London during World War II, became the respected voice of the military. For Murrow, as was the case with most broadcasters, the war in Korea was a test of strength between the major nations, and while supportive, they were surprisingly open about military difficulties.

The radio was active on the front line as the government provided both news and entertainment to be picked up by the troops when possible. These were simple reports with the effort directed as much at propaganda as it was as entertainment. In Korea the enemy provided its own brand of news broadcast to the United Nations, consisting primarily of songs and comments by Seoul City Sue, an American broadcasting for the communists.[10]

During the war the production companies tired to provide some in-depth coverage, and such programs as *The Radio* were the primary source of information available. Even before *See It Now*, Murrow provided an anxious voice witnessing the struggle. He did two special Christmas broadcasts—Christmas in Korea, 1952–1953—in which he tried to close the gap in understanding between the war and the home front. Others less political in their inquiries pushed for home front awareness and supported civilian aid by such things as blood donor programs. Several programs used the war as background for USO-type presentations, though there was very little original music created for such events.

In many cases the radio coverage was stymied by the lack of communication facilities available to the journalists in Korea or Japan. The radio correspondent, it was often suggested, was involved in "censorship without a war," and the effect was that little coverage was conducted. The need for daily delivery of material meant that lot of frontline reporting was a rehash of the military briefing provided. Some direct reporting was tried but was generally not successful. For example, Ensign Jack Seigal provided a moment-by-moment coverage of the invasion of Wolmi-do in September 1950.

The war was no more big news for the radio broadcasters than it was for the print media. E.R. Murrow, writing at the beginning of the war, might well have reflected the end of the fight when he reported, "The first nine weeks of direct radio coverage of the Korean War was considered conspicuous by its scarcity." The armistice hearings, for example, were covered by one journalist, Leroy Hanson, who had to use an army field telephone to report it. Postwar coverage was nearly nonexistent.

Magazines

To a large extent periodical magazines were the best source of information about the war. During the combat years, *Time Magazine* reached an audience of 8.1 million, and *Life Magazine* circulation grew until on one occasion they published more than 13.5 million copies. A lot of "news" magazines existed and more arrived during the war, but they did not provide any unusual amount of coverage. *Life, Look, Time, Everybody's Magazine, Popular Mechanics, Saturday Evening Post*, and other magazines were a source of specialized stories and more and more photographs as they became available. The initial reporting of those U.S. magazines came from correspondents on the ground and the coverage was broad and inquisitive. They reported on troops firing on civilians, on disorganized retreats, and on violence of all kinds that particularly reflected on South Korean troops. This quickly changed as the government moved in quickly to protect what little positive image remained. Within six weeks censorship was on.

Life magazine makes an interesting example of how the coverage worked out. What was true for it was basically true for all. During the first few weeks of combat, *Life* was dedicated to a weekly news story about the war, and several features relating to it. But by October 1950 the coverage began to lessen and fewer and fewer articles or features appeared. Several editions showed up without any mention of the war at all. The Letters to the Editor column that had reflected the public response to their coverage suddenly, in November 1950, went dry with few and then no letters appearing. After late November 1950 and into 1951 coverage continued, but less and less was being reported. By the time the war concluded, discussion of it had decreased and began to fade away.[11]

During the war the cartoon was probably the most reflective of the national mood and attitude. While the popular press reported features, photojournalism and short-cut analysis of the events, cartoons appear to have been more in touch with the public lack of interest. The academics never seemed to get interested. Serious study of the war as it was going on had little appeal, and in the first thirty years following the war, only one article on veterans was published in the most popular of periodicals, the *New York Times*.

Television

Television was just coming into its own, and at this point a newscaster was little more than a person sitting at a desk reading the paper. The war was the first test for the up-and-coming television industry, but Korean was not in any sense a television war. The equipment was not technically capable, or the staffs professionally sophisticated enough to provide television reporting. What was needed was a new breed of journalists who had been taught the use of visual materials. By 1950 what little visual material they had available was simply a replay of the newsreels. As late at 1957, critics of the industry were saying that the visual understanding was at a standstill and needed to start again. There were few television sets in people's homes, and where there was one, only a few of the owners were interested in news broadcasts.

This does not mean that the TV was without impact. It was on *Front Line Camera* on 25 July 1950 that President Truman moved Americans from observations of a civil war between two strong-willed Korean governments to a crusade to protect the Republic of Korea and the freedom of the American people. It played a role in associating the events in Korea with the expanding fear of domestic communism. The McCarthy headings became daytime TV for many.

During the war, the visual coverage improved, but at no time was the industry technically capable or deeply experienced enough to provide valid coverage. The reporting of World War II that was done via radio was a matter of summarizing battles and providing analysis, but TV reporting was far more demanding, requiring fresh supplies of battle film on a daily basis. In this demand the TV stations relied on newsreel film crews, or more and more on the U.S. Army Signal Corps. While these films were helpful, they were not taken with journalistic standards, but rather with a full military agenda. That is to say, they provided America what the military wanted Americans to see.

It is also significant to acknowledge that TV crews, vastly different from the dog-faced front-line correspondent of World War II, required vast amounts of equipment, thus help from the army for transportation, even for the basic necessities, thus bringing their objectivity into question. As well, TV news was itself subject to military censorship, a move that was generally accepted by journalists seeing it as a means to equalize the breaking of important stories.

What was provided in these early TV efforts was a highly sensational view of the war that focused on the anti-communistic struggle. This was best presented in *Telenews Weekly* (Hearst Productions) and *Front Line Camera*. These inexperienced and not always accurate reporters were responsible in many ways for the myths that grew, including the incalculable significance of American air power, the near invincibility of the United States pilots, and the technological excellence of the American military man who was dedicated to freedom. One such report is typical of the mood and attitude. "As Communist forces lower an Iron Curtain over conquered areas, instituting Marxist reforms and bringing their brand of democracy to once-free Korea, United States answers communism's program of lies and promises."[12]

The TV coverage, like much of the broadcast coverage of the war, was unimpressive and even boring. Edward R. Murrow, perhaps more than anyone else reporting, did his best to present the war in some sort of neutral context, but even his influence was vastly limited.

Cooking Without Taste Buds

The Korean War is suffering its share of the difficulties caused by the fact the historical community has drifted off track in some serious respects and is not addressing many of the historical topics of this time. Our universities seem to have bred a new generation of basically rudderless historians. That is, men and women who research, write, and teach without having considered the basic core assumptions of history, or even of themselves. They are trying to function with little or no philosophy of history. To an amazing degree they have failed in the primary task of evaluating their own discipline.

Divorced from any general theory on the operation of their discipline, many have slipped further and further down the slippery slope into sociology. They have thus become more interested in providing an explanation than they are in offering any comprehension or understanding of the event involved. They appear to be more interested in the social context of behavior than they are of evaluating events against behavior and contingencies. They have become disciples of social concourse and thus have failed in their initial task.

Historians who study and analyze with no primary assumption about the nature of history itself will write reports rather than investigative and insightful narratives. So far the profession has done little to provide the much-needed historical analysis that can free the veteran and the people's response from some of the ambiguity of this war. While there is some very fine historical writing available, there are as well a lot of apathetic inquiries based on myths and written traditions that reflect a poor understanding of the meaning of history itself. Having started depicting their reconstruction of the events with much too broad a brush, these would-be historians have been making the assumption that they can write history without reading the directions.

To put it in somewhat different terms, there is the need to acknowledge that the discipline of history has been suffering from the bifurcation of methods and thus an adjustment of goals. Many historians seem to be facing decisions about fact and pattern that leave them either heading down the unfamiliar path to reductionism on their way to sociology or they attach themselves to the social sciences. Or, on the other hand, they are being easily seduced by the apparent variations of sensitive history in search of a political correctness of meaning and the potential of final answers.

The problem has been coming on for some time. Historians have reached that point where they think they no longer have to test their tools. Like the observer at a powerful telescope who had a speck of dust in his eye, it is necessary to account for those things they know need adjustment, maybe even a compromise, to account for failures in the researcher. That is to say, they do not consider a philosophy of history by which to understand the speck, the assumption, in their own historical eye. They do not teach it in the graduate schools, they do not talk about it at their conferences, they do not write about it in their journals; in fact, most historians these days act as if they had been born with such a level of comprehension they no longer need to consider the implications of their own assumptions.

This lack of primary self-analysis means the historian has no core against which to challenge his inquiry. Many a historian feels capable of operating from a self-designed cloud of objectivity, a powerful assumption that his limited experience qualifies him to challenge the impact of tradition and contingency. A dangerous thought.

The British historian Edward H. Carr says it clearly: "Those historians who today pretend to dispense with a philosophy of history are merely trying vainly and self-consciously, like members of a nudist colony, to recreate a Garden of Eden in their garden suburb."[13] Because of this, much of what has been assumed to be the objectivity of facts accumulated about this unknown war are grossly mistaken. What is often recorded is not what was remembered. The myths used to explain the unexplained, and the justifications designed to justify the ironic, have quite easily become the record, and as such tell us so little of the real story. Among other dangers is the inability to acknowledge that memories are primarily based on feelings, not on events. A good many of the works available are products of the assumptions from World War II, or highly spiced by some post–Vietnam rhetoric. Writing as they often do from the revisionist assumptions of postwar comprehension, and trying to research from postwar historical and political theory, they are as foolish as the lawyer who is his own client. What seems to be lacking in so many efforts, amateur and professional, is some understanding of what can be learned from history and what cannot.

The prime concern, however, is the effect on the nature of history and how it relates to the narrative of the Korean War. The shifting outlook of the historian, and the failure of many to use the more majestic tools of the discipline, have taken the historian into the heavily mined territory of sociology. And while it may well be an honorable profession, it is too focused on commonality and precision to be historical. The term "social science" is sometimes used interchangeably with sociology, but it is different. It is intended to identify the specific science of society. Or more generally the term is used to mean all other disciplines that science will not claim. It therefore assumes a common denominator with all other areas of knowledge, from jurisprudence to husbandry, without fully understanding any of them.

In their inquiry the historian is in the enviable position of viewing information with selectivity, simultaneity, and a shifting of scale. What this means is that he can withdraw from the stream of events and at the same time continue to move in and out of the effects of the event. Back and forth between macroscopic and microscopic analysis, like the time traveler, the historian imposes significance on the past. Since the historian remains in the present as he explores the past, it is the historian who gets to select what in the past is worth our investigation. The tendency is to model the past on the present. That is, he finds significant in the past those things he believes are significant now. In so doing he must avoid the tendency to simply model the past on what is important today. The tendency is to believe that today is somehow evidence of yesterday's behavior, a tendency loaded with mistakes.

Consider for a moment the impact of the contingency that is always present, thus never considered. Think of the "causes" for the behavior of the Korean War soldier. It may well not be an earth-shaking decision, the enemy's preparation, nor careless military leadership, but rather some apparently insignificant contingency, some unexpected some-

thing that comes along, and according to Murphy's Law, changes everything. What comes to mind immediately in the case of Korea is the 40-
degree drop in temperature for men still wearing summer uniforms.
Few have managed to capture the magnitude of "causes" by which the
situation of this war was significantly altered by the impact of the cold
on the individual.[14] The weather's arbitrary behavior is often one of the
many unconsidered events.

Consider as well scale shifting. Sounding like something out of mys-
ticism, it is little more than the opportunity to shift points of view, to
look at something from a variety of angles not available to the witness or
the participant. The narrative, the illustrative anecdote, is the basic tool
of the historian, and when he uses a particular event to propose a general point, or to alter a traditional point of view, scale shifting has taken
place. The more easily described smaller point is used to describe the
character of the larger. But for this to work, the craftsman must be prepared to consider how a phenomenon so small as to escape notice could
in time shape events so large we continue to wonder why they occurred.
Such a view crosses not only over time and space, but also in the location of our inquiry. The latter offers the ability to be in several places at
once, to see events and procedures that were not then visible but are now.

There is a current unwillingness in narrative history to take the
broader views, to avoid the single source of a potential assumption,
and this lends its weight to the invalidity of understanding. The historian can see the battle from both sides. Unlike those participating in
the battle, he has greater vision when he brings to bear the ability to
shift the scale of the investigation from the macroscopic to the microscopic and back again.

Today's historian is facing yet another interesting attack on the
purity of the discipline. In history and sociology it is called "emotional
sensitivity."[15] People who hold this view believe that the way a particular
society channeled and displayed their feelings has profoundly affected
both national and individual life. They offer the view that the emotions
and the conventions regulate our understanding of the society's values,
identities, and ideological commitments, and thus history.[16]

By definition, emotional sensitivity imposes on the deeply personal
experience, particularly when it is seen in deviance from the social
norm. In this case those who are sensitive are not the historians but
those being studied. The historian theoretically is not sensitive to the

emotional impact of the facts upon the observer. The impact is not in the story, but rather in how it is received by those involved. Such persons might include migrants, or older citizens, or religious believers who will be harmed by hearing something they don't want to know.

J.H. Flaskerud and B.I. Winslow are the gurus who suggest that "when designing research on sensitive topics it is important to weigh the potential risk against the benefits by giving careful consideration to whether the research findings might further stigmatize or marginalize the population under study."[17] This concern supports both the advance of such historical efforts previously believed to be too sensitive for our investigation (sexual practices, religion, incest, violence), and second to take the sensitive in to the study with us. That is to develop a personal relationship with those being studied. This is true even up to and including the point of personal connections. The sensitivity then is not to what is discovered, but to the gatekeepers (ethical committees and research planning teams) who must determine the risk of what is concluded from such highly emotional subjects.

While such an idea might be great for a Sunday School class, it is historical nonsense. First of all, one must be aware that it is totally implausible, and is little other than a reaction to the growth of technological advances that focus on the asking of questions, not the answering of them. And, of course, it results from the beliefs of some who think that they are adept at "arriving at history's truth" without mitigating any threat of harm to the partisans involved. The tendency to be effected by such a thesis has led some current historians to release what seems to be soulless history.

Perhaps a more basic problem for the historian is what academics call reductionism: the methodological process by which sociologists, and occasionally a historian, can provide the explanation for an entire event by providing explanations of the individual parts of the whole. The explanations for the totality of a system, they believe, can be understood by an analysis of the numerous parts that are involved, much like when you take the toaster apart to see what makes it work. This view would make some sense if, like the toaster, history were composed of a given number of events and we could know them. The final key is the affirmation that the total is the sum of its parts. Such a belief is not history, it is sociology, thus it fails to support the generally held assumption among historians that the whole is more than a sum of its parts.

The alternative approach stands in contrast to this view and is identified as holism. This broad term identifies the belief that while systems and events can have emergent properties as a whole, they are not explained from a sum of their parts. The Principle of Holism was concisely summarized by the philosopher Aristotle in his work *Metaphysics*: "The whole is more than the sum of the parts." Alfred North Whitehead, contemporary philosopher speaking in opposition to reductionism, called it the "fallacy of the misplaced concreteness." Sven Erik Jorgensen further seeks to avoid reductionism and suggests some systems are so complex that it would never be possible to describe all their details. Referring to the Heisenberg uncertainty principle[18] in physics, he argues that most relevant ecological phenomena are altered by the fact they are being investigated.[19]

Perhaps as a side effect of reductionism, there appears as well some sort of fascination with lesser things. The Korean War, fought for three long years, is most often written about as if it lasted only until the retreat at Chosin. Hundreds of significant battles, unit actions, even operations fail to draw any attention away from yet another heroic description of Inchon or the magnificent retreat from the Reservoir. The war was a daily event, each day having some effect on the outcome. The study of the war must somehow capture the mood, if not the facts, of this truth and go beyond detailed descriptions of single, often unrelated, events.

One characteristic of the move toward the socialization of the historical profession has been the rise of what is often called the Nostradamus Complex. That is, many historians of the Korean War seem to be suffering from the need to identify the past as a means of predicting the future. Assuming causal relations that will move the reader from the wart on Cleopatra's nose to the prediction of Kim Jong Un's warlike intentions is attractive but very dangerous indeed. When you try to explain the present by constructions of the past, the "cloistered soothsayer" has set themselves up for failure. Famed British historian R.G. Collingwood says that "whenever historians claim to be able to determine the future in advance of its happening we may know with certainty that something has gone wrong with their fundamental conception of history." In the main they are more interested in foretelling than in retelling. In this case, they are more anxious to prove the war in Korea was the cause of the Vietnam War than dealing with it in its own right.

And in this interest, they are quick to read the present into formulating a past that will meet their criteria. Their assertions of cause and effect, presented without overlying theory or comprehension, leads them to interpret events, and criticize leadership, on the basis of knowing things that they in fact could not possibly know.[20]

The discipline is suffering from too much reliance on the reductionist method, using it as a way to generalize about the past. It seeks to remove from the causal chain of events one that would alter the outcome of them all. Reductionism implies therefore that there are actually independent variables and that we can know what they are. But contrary to the vision of some social scientists, human behavior—that is, history—is not subject to the working of rules or even trends that can be so verified. Certainly not to the point of forecasting the future. David Halberstam's *The Coldest Winter* (2008) is a near-perfect example of this inclination as he tends to find a Vietnam result for every Korean War decision. Revisionist Bruce Cumings points out that Halberstam made all the classic mistakes that popular American historians have been making about this little-understood war.[21]

Waiting in the wings to expand this problem of sources is the loss of those "bits of paper"—those notes, and comments, and recollections scratched down for later use and released in time to the mainstream of research. It should come as no great surprise to anyone that the abundance of communication has had the effect of making it harder and harder to prioritize what is "relevant information," and more importantly, has removed the source of much of our information. While it may be possible to go back and read everyone's e-mails it is less and less possible to trace the development of an idea, or the provenance of a thesis. The background materials, the pages and pages of handwritten notes, are in danger of being lost to the assumed universality of the "cloud."

Paramount to the military concern about their own history is the fact that the army, for example, is losing its own records and they are not sure what to do about it. For the last decade or so the military is not really sure where it has been, who was there, or what they did. Like the nation, it became difficult to keep track of. In 2013 or so the military became aware that they could not produce the highly detailed official histories for this period as they had for previous wars, simply because most of the memory had been reduced to after-action reports, anecdotes, reminiscences, and a citation or two from mail sent but long forgotten. These tend to have the memory of outcome rather than preparation and thus are only partially remembered.

Sooner or later the ambitious historian must go beyond the secondary and public historian who continues to ignore vast collections of materials related to this war. As an example, take the Center for the Study of the Korean War in Independence, Missouri, that has, for more than twenty-five years, been a major depository for Korean War documents, archives, and photographic evidence of this war. And yet a casual check of the researchers who have written on the war suggests that many of those so engaged did not visit or use the facilities. Hundreds of thousands of documents have been left untouched.

And last—and some might conclude this is the last straw in the hope for a more objective history—is the weak position of or even lack of a revisionist tradition. That is, the academic inquiry into the war has not yet been challenged by the criticism of traditional revisionism. Historical consideration of an event like the Korean War has phases that can be identified. The process, reflecting the Hegelian triad—thesis-antithesis-synthesis—is often referred to as orthodox and revisionist history. During and immediately after the war, several volumes were published describing what happened and establishing a sort of traditional or orthodox view. Then some years after that, other historians reviewed the work and altered the traditional view, revising it with new information and interpretation.

Because of the lack of interest in the war, very little of this secondary phase of revision has taken place. Generally the best information is fostered by this process happening over and over again. While some are skeptical of the revisionist label, it should not be regarded as pejorative. The old categories of traditionalist (or orthodox) and revision have their limits, but they remain accurate and useful. Since the early 1980s, concern and the rather unexpected availability of substantial documentation from both the Chinese and the Soviet Union should have produced a whole new set of revisionist histories.

Where Were You, John Wayne?

In terms of their responsibility for reflecting the culture in which they exist, the movie industry has not done well. The most that can be said is that while films have always had the ability to look back and reflect on our times, in this case they allow themselves to become a part of the problem. That is to say that their behavior reflected the general apathy concerning the war. So rather than delivering some potential meaning or memory to the Korean War, they simply used it for a while and dropped it. The fact that John Wayne did not make a Korean War movie tells us a lot about Hollywood and their view of the war. Wayne, the composite American warrior, did not want to make a movie about America at its weakest, so instead produced and starred in *The Alamo*, which paid tribute to the republican American character that he wished to encourage.[22]

Overall the lack of interest in what might well have been booked as a unique war is somewhat puzzling, for in most cases films about wars are created as an opportunity to identify American values and the courage and dedication of its people. In the end Hollywood did not see in Korea the full measure of those truths that described the generation that went to war a decade earlier.

Some years ago, before the History Channel sold out to reality TV, the producers aired a discussion between some recognized historians and those who had worked with the popular series *M*A*S*H*. No one disagreed that the comedy was primarily a protest against the war in Vietnam, and not an effort to remember Korea. Earlier efforts based on the original 1968 book by Richard Hooker and Robert Altman's 1970 film of the same name were much more geared to comedy and social satire than political commentary. While both were popular it was the TV program that the Library of Congress considered "socially significant" enough to preserve.[23] Thus while the producers defended themselves on the show's historical accuracy, they also admitted that they had altered what they knew about the war in order to focus their protest against what was happening. They not only made little effort to identify the Korean event, they deliberately altered the history to support their analysis of another war.

Those who wrote and appeared in *M*A*S*H* were hostile to the war as well as the army, served under protest, saw no significance in the conflict, and so focused on the absurdity of war itself, and thus misled the nation (intentionally or not) into a false impression of the events and participants of the Korean War. This does not provide us an adequate picture at all. The difficulties, however, go far beyond this misrepresentation, for the very presence of the series in the minds of most Americans have provided a totally different focus on war.

It is only fair, however, to acknowledge that the industry serves several markets. What is produced is generally what sells. Whatever degree they should go to beyond that to alter social understanding is a matter of opinion, but in the past there is every evidence they have done a better job.

The objections are easy to identify, beginning with the fact that there were few films produced; Hollywood's reading of the market was simple: no one was interested. More than six times as many films have been made about the Vietnam war. The events of the Korean War, fought with World War II weapons and uniforms, were not all that different. Nevertheless it quickly became the source of B-grade movies with little-known actors. The war did not provide either a cliché of national patriotism or a final victory to celebrate. The events in Korea fell into that ambiguous middle ground of history that tended to make a mockery of America's long-held Jacksonian belief in "unconditional surrender."

With very few exceptions the films produced about this war were of lesser quality. Hollywood knows how to make great films, and *Pork Chop Hill* and *Steel Helmet* came very close. But most were not quality, and a series of dreadful and equally forgetful movies appeared, none worse perhaps than *The Nun and the Sergeant*, which illustrated the extent to which Hollywood would go in the name of sales. Most of these cheap and unmarketable films drifted off to be lost in storage vaults.

The industry quickly produced its own stereotypes. It chose to maintain, and in some cases extrapolate, the myths of World War II, but did so under the pressure and assumptions of its own era. A creeping depiction emerged of the soldier as more angry than patriotic, more anti-authoritarian than was the case, more apathetic than energetic, and with unexplained hints at an underlying weakness.[24]

An interesting look at the changing nature of the display of the American warrior is found in the controversy over Clint Eastwood's *Heartbreak Ridge*. Named after a Korean event, it focuses on a Marine drill instructor who finally leads his men into battle in Granada. The controversy was that the Army refused to help in production. The Marines withdrew help and the Defense Department divorced itself from the production. The argument was expressed by the army spokes-man who said that both Eastwood and the film displayed a stereotype of the armed forces that reflected World War II and Korea but not the modern army. Hard-drinking, tough, even mean at times, Eastwood reflected an earlier period in military history and not one that the army wanted to carry on.

Hollywood films tended to follow the eight- to ten-man squad in which the military was characterized by diversity. Usually you could find the soft-hearted and overly sensitive young man who was going to be a writer, the dumb one who never knew what it was all about, a bright natural leader, at least one from Brooklyn, and a variety of lesser soldiers who were available to be killed off during the film if necessary. The men reflected what the producers thought were diversified Amer-icans, and in some combination tried to cover the basic types: a white bigoted southerner, a Latino, the lover, the career soldier, a liberal, one who was overly patriotic, an Oriental, a religious zealot, and more reflective of the 1960s than the 1950s, they depicted at least one black man (usually strong and arrogant).

The story lines adopted reflect little imagination, taking stories of the traditional military images. Surrounded by what passed for military jargon, they mimicked World War II. In some cases producers did not even bother to update the combat footage. Having successfully told the World War II story, screenwriters took full advantage of already-written material and carried on a World War II background to provide the plot for a lot of Korean films. Memories of earlier battles, psychological baggage real or imagined, as appeared in *Battle Hymn* (1967), *Torpedo Alley* (1952), and *Battle Zone* (1952), all addressed the problems of the retreads who found themselves back in combat.

For those seeking to branch out in some way, the focus was nar-rowed to prisoners of war. Well over 60 percent of the films made included the role of the POW as a significant part of the story. Holly-wood expedited the idea that POWs in general and the individual sol-diers in particular were being brainwashed and had in some fashion betrayed their comrades and their county by showing a weakness. The popular theme was a totally unfair description of the Korean War vet-erans. Watching Hollywood's struggle with plot development, one might wonder at the number of prisoners taken, for the impression is that there were more perhaps than were actually taken. The plight of the POW became the marketable theme of Hollywood's enterprise and defection became the key. Those responsible apparently did not agree with Christopher Wilson, American historian writing in 2016: "The obligation of any film using history as its source is not to get at the truth, and certainly not at the whole truth, but to get at a truth."[25]

Several excellent stories from this war have been bypassed. These include the masterful biological expert who went behind enemy lines to see if germ weapons had actually been used, the last stand of the Gloucestershire Regiment, or even the landing at Wonson that would make a great comedy. The famed Inchon landing (about which only one movie was actually made)[26] or the Chosin Retreat were points of glorification. It is not the lack of good stories, or accounts of personal adventures, or behind-the-scenes disagreement, that prevents good movies being made.

The available stories were weak, and besides, most of the movie public had already seen many of them. The search for the unique led to the decision to focus on the impact of brainwashing. A story was to be found in the assumed effects and successes of communist brain control. Real or not, the theme provided the ground of suspicion needed to spruce up the Korean War film. Many of those involved in the war were pictured as pawns in individual trials where their behavior had been in question. War films moved the "escape at any cost" scenario of the World War II prisoner of war movie, to the "what can we do about it?" reaction. The lack of escape attempts focused on the implied individual weakness and vulnerability of the citizen-soldier.[27]

Hollywood was well aware that the portrayal of the harsh treatment and torture of prisoners was depressing, and that the deliberate attempt to blame the prisoners at large would be seen as callous. Their clever response was to make films once removed from the action: the courtroom trial. The fact is that, contrary to the suggestion set off by Hollywood, there were very few trials indeed. Out of the 4,428 men who had been prisoners and had returned to the United States, only 565 were even questioned about their behavior during imprisonment and no charges were leveled. Only fourteen of the POWs considered suspicious ever went to trial. Most of the 23 defectors returned to the United States or some other Western nation and were quickly absorbed. Part of this low number was created by the military itself. In their haste to disown the traitors, they had dishonorably discharged the "turncoats" from the service. What this meant in the long run was that when they returned they were no longer under military jurisdiction and free from any punishment.

The belief in collaboration was, in fact, too traumatic to be ignored, even in film entertainment. *The Bamboo Prison* (1957) and *Sergeant Ryker* (1968) are but two of the dozen or so examples. However, loyalty, patriotism and commercial savvy encouraged producers to make films that would guide and reassure the audience during this time, and the dark topics needed a cushion. Eventually the film makers settled on trying to have it both ways. The films paralleled the development of public sentiment where the initial shock at collaboration prompted an examination of captivity. This was followed by greater sensitivity designed to replace disillusionment. The movies even created something of a backlash and an effort was made to mend the fences somewhat. The best effort was *The Rack*, which informed a humiliated nation that a solution to the POW disgrace had already been worked out. It was to be found in the rededication to traditional values brought about by more training, and the depth of values taught to the soldiers. In the final analysis, those who collaborated were more to be pitied than to be scorned.

The public quickly mimicked Hollywood's response. American youth in captivity became a staple topic for discussions at civic events where patriotic speakers lamented the deterioration of morals, and indirectly the failure of the armed services. Charles Mayer, military psychiatrist, became a leader in this movement, attacking a lack of faith in America, a poor education, a lack of toughness, wishy-washy mothers spoiling their sons, all of which were to blame for the decline in national spirit. What is so compelling about the role of the prisoner in these films is that the image of their weakness is melded into all aspects of the war. They were weak people, not just weak warriors.

The suspicion broadened. These flawed products of a soft America were considered not only weak themselves, but they were susceptible to brainwashing, an idea that caught the American fantasy. These men who had been brainwashed were not just obedient to their captors, but they had become believers. No better illustration of this is available than the film *The Manchurian Candidate* (1962). The title became a term that quickly caught on and was used by most with little to no understanding of what they were talking about. The success of this particular film is an indication of just how deeply the fear of being captured and revamped actually frightened Americans. The thesis that emerged was one in which the Korean War POWs were especially susceptible to collaboration. It was later debunked by the military but by then the wide brush of criticism had tainted all the servicemen.

For a nation whose resolve was called into question by the lack of victory, it appeared that in Korea—unlike Vietnam, where films suggested the nation had betrayed the POW—the POW had betrayed the nation. These men were depicted as weak, and as they began to return home after their captivity, the media identified them as traitors and accused many of having turned to communism. In later Vietnam films the POWs, who had been double-crossed by government agents and the media as well as frightened politicians, returned to the war in a series of *Rambo* films to save themselves.[28] There have been no such Korean heroes.

Expressing any popular sympathy for the man who had been a prisoner was seen as a lack of personal loyalty, what the Advisory Committee on Prisoners of War referred to as "misguided public sympathy." Some were willing to suggest that it might be better to pity the ex–POW than it was to pass judgment on him. But just as many claimed that empathy for such cowards simply made them weaker. Sympathy just got in the way and what was needed was more discipline. Right or wrong, the awful acknowledgment that good honest men can give in, even without physical pain, challenged the narrative upon which was the moral fiber of America was built.

Good or bad, right or wrong, the Korean War film once initiated has generally disappeared from the public domain. Sounding very much like a Yogi Berraism[29] is the fact that the Korean War movies, as bad as they were, have gone away. Not only have the producers stopped making them, but they are not distributing the ones that they made. Unlike World War II films, one of which is always showing someplace on late-night TV, films depicting the Korean War are not available. At least, if they were still around, that might remind someone that the war was fought. The duration of interest in the war was limited and apparently had been reached, as far as the film market was concerned. World War II, with its purity of intent and execution, remains strong. Vietnam films, with their background of domestic unrest, are abundant. But when it comes to adventure films, Marvel Comics has pretty much taken over.

As far as the filmmakers were concerned, America's purpose in fighting this war remained in question. Even those films that were produced are inclined, without exception, to express a national crisis of confidence, and to do so does not serve well as either patriotism nor entertainment. In these limited productions there is a clearly defined move from romantic nationalism to nihilistic individualism, and the corresponding journey from emotional expression to detachment. Hollywood's misinterpretation of the Korean War not only killed the desire for more movies on the subject, it provoked a generally false idea of what happened there.

There is another subtle feature seen in the Korean War film, and that is the degree to which the wound has gradually moved from being a "Red Badge of Courage" to being a ticket home. In a striking difference from earlier accounts, Korean War films graphically exposed wounds in which pain was acknowledged, and personal concern was reflected, but generally within the area of escaping additional risk. Wounded men were depicted in their anger and were almost void of any interest in what was happening to their buddies. In the main, these films placed the responsibility for the pain on the persons in pain, often blaming a mystic happenstance for its occurrence. The response generally reflected a sense of gratitude for the "million-dollar wound" that was just bad enough. But anger seemed to be the key word. Unlike the films of other wars, pain appears to be something that needed to be aggressively fought, but was itself an incitement to violence. As one solder put it, "Pain filled him with the intense desire to kill those fucking bastards."[30]

This idea is investigated at some length by the British academician Joanna Bourkes.[31] She recognizes that pain is both physical and emotional and that the emotional state—thus the pain itself—is reflected in the times and attitudes. The manner in which it is depicted in both memorials and literature reflects the cultural as well as the individual response. And thus, the character of the war, those who fought it, and those who interpreted it, have changed over the years. In any case, this war has pictured body pain in a different pattern than various other wars in which we have been engaged.

Historically many early societies depicted the wound as a sacrifice for the greater good, an honor to receive, and the continuing discomfort from the wound was to be seen as a lasting engagement of personal sacrifice. The honor was reflected not only in the patriotic character of the person harmed, but in the responses of his or her comrades. It was evidence of national values.

In the Civil War, the correlation between the wound and the description of the pain involved was something less a recording of national pride than it was dealing with the regret, even the inconvenience of the wound. Interestingly, it is also to be noted that in many cases the wounded soldiers are described as apologizing for the trouble their wound is causing those caring for them.

Detachment was the characteristic of the wounded soldier in World War I and to some extent World War II. This detachment is not a separation from either patriotism or nationalism, but rather the sense of acceptance, and is portrayed in responses that were often described as striking understatements. Wounds were accepted as the cost of battle, and while there is some merit in identifying the event as a sacrifice for the cause of the nation, it did not require a great deal of attention. Between the world wars and during the long spell of relative peace, something changed, and this indifference was replaced by a far more individualistic approach. The expressions of patriotic sacrifice were greatly lessened, and whatever national or even moral value might be identified, the most striking condition depicted was the drastic movement from romance to nihilistic individualism.

The long search for some special meaning in Hollywood's approach to the Korean War fails to provide much insight. The author Jeanine Basinger, in writing about the subject, came to the well-supported conclusion that the "format of the Korean War film was definitely a replay of the World War II combat film," with little other than the introduction of the communists, primarily the Russians, as the chief enemy. Maybe, some have speculated, they are just no better nor any worse than the war movies generally produced. Whatever the reason, they paint a distorted picture of the war and those who fought it.

Certainly there is a close relationship between Hollywood's willingness to give credence to the mythos of America's past and the later accusations that entertainers who questioned the nobility of the U.S. past were "pinko-commies" or outright communists. Particular investigations into Hollywood personalities by the House Un-American Activities Committee resulted in threats and blacklists that greatly affected the movie business.[32]

117

The Empty Shelves

The vast silence that represents the Korean War is quickly illustrated by the empty shelves in the history section of the bookstore or by the lack of musical scores for memorial symphonies found at music libraries. It can be illustrated by the absence of novels and plays or by the lack of paintings hanging in the galleries of art. Those who go in search of a cultural response to the Korean War will find little evidence, and even less indication of passion and high quality. It is, in terms of memory and creative stimuli, a national tragedy.

One cannot be clear about the cause-and-effect relationship, but at first it seems astonishing. Perhaps the war was of such low intensity it unleashed no creative initiative. Or perhaps the war was fought by those lacking in graphic interest and so its events were not seen through the eyes of the artisan. Or perhaps it is the opposite: the lack of cultural icons has made the war difficult to remember. It is, some have said, a lack of market, but the degree to which that is true has not been well tested.

For whatever reason, from the lack of press coverage through the war to the near absence of reflective literature, those whose responsibility it is to focus our heritage have in this case failed to do so. The historical community has recorded the war far too quickly and often too subjectively, providing questionable narrative and ineffective analysis. The movie industry, a traditional tool for pubic memory and commemoration, has not only failed to produce the sort of film needed, but has contributed to the misconceptions by ill-conceived tales poorly told. Yet what is so surprising is just how few novels and poetry have been produced.

World Wars I and II produced a lot of war-related novels. There was some early concern that the postwar distractions of magazines, radio, movies and even the emergence of television would limit the number, but it did not appear to do so. Others speculated that the end of the war might forecast an end to the obsolete, dull, and generally useless pastime of reading military novels. Some even suggested that the end of such writing was in sight because of the poor quality of much of what had written about World War II. But that has not been the case. While the genre has not produced the high quality of work that the experts seek, the market continues, spurred on once in awhile by novels by James Jones, Norman Mailer, and perhaps the carryover of Ernest Hemingway. The novels of World Wars I and II and Vietnam have survived, but not really those from Korea.

While the myth has generally been held that the Korean War produced as many novels as did other wars, it also suggested the novel was making a lasting contribution to the canon of American literature. These views are unfounded. The idea that somehow the war is better understood because of the unique body of information provided by the novel is misleading, even when expressed by recognized critics. The idea that novels of the Korean War appeared, and continued to do so at the same rate as other wars, is wrong. What seems equally wrong is that no one seems to have noticed.

The cupboard is empty, and because of this, the literary community has failed to assume its social responsibility to aid the society in confronting the mixed and confusing nature of war. Not only of war, but of this war in particular. What little is available can pretty much be defined as nondecisive and lacking the confrontation typical of the periods between World War II and Vietnam. It is difficult not to agree with Spencer Tetley, who wrote: "I know of no great novel written about it. And there was no poetry written. No songs. Nothing on the cultural side marks the passage of Korea. It was basically over and done with and forgotten." If anything, the absence seems to provide a perspective on the Americans' limited response and restrained reaction of the war itself.

Granted, there was little general interest in Asia. While the political significance of the area was not lost on those in command, the wider interest was far more focused on what was happening in Europe. The same was true for the American people. Even after the occupation of Japan, and the creation of some more informed citizens, Asia did not offer the variety of experiences or the extremes of circumstances that lent themselves to the production of plots and adventures as did the European nations.

The bulk of what has been written is about the ground troops on the line. The circumstance gives the author a daily source of events with which to react. The army carried the brunt of the war and provided most of the experiences upon which the novelist might build a story. With some exceptions the majority of these novels deal with the front line, the front, the MLR (Main Line of Resistance), and the early movement of troops. Unlike World War II, there are no well-known novels of the airborne troops in Korea. Very few are about the navy, only one about the submarine service, and the largest number are semi-autobiographical.

The life of the grunt offered a sound basis for setting the stage of the war as well as the fact that most of the participant-novelists (those who took part in the war) were veterans of some ground unit. In general the themes reflected on the isolation of war and of this war in particular. Many combined this with a subplot of growing up in public. They focused on what Curt Andes, in his novel *The Price of Courage* (1957), calls "the terrible loneliness of being shot at."[33] They tended to center on the individual soldier, though some group heroes were introduced, or they confronted the military as an institution. In the early sixties there was a brief new interest in the army's role in the Korean War, but these few works that were considered prominent during that time were really little more than a rephrasing of previously presented treatments.[34]

The Marines, as might be expected, are the prime force in a disproportionate number of novels of Korea. A good many of these were written by career warriors and official historians who were themselves Marines. As combat troops, the Marines appear to be far more popular, and the simple location of the action within the Corps gives it an air of mystery and commitment. This is in part because they were good fighters, and because they maintained a professional spirit administered by the Corps headquarters that created a culture of the exalted warrior. The novels reflect the same bellicose attitude toward civilians and the noncombatant as do most military novels. These works often seem extreme and do not always reflect events as they were. Of those that appeared, Martin Russ's *The Last Parallel* (1957) probably has as much to do with this exaggerated view of the Marines as anything. This is true as well of James Brady's *The Marines of Autumn*. The great exception of this is Pat Frank's *Hold Back the Night*, in which the Marines are so low-key that it might as well be an army novel.

Only a handful of novels relate to the war at sea or in the air. For example, World War II produced more than 100 fairly good novels based on the submarine service, but while subs were in action in Korea, only one work appears. The sea war was harsh and dangerous and provided more than enough action to carry a novel, but most sailors faced routine daily activities and only sporadic action that made a consistent story difficult. The same was true for the Air Force, which fought in short stressful missions and then spent the rest of the time waiting for the next assignment. A few novels have been able to grab the context of such worlds. Clandestine efforts appeared to be popular plots, though in some cases they are so implausible as to be funny.

Among the novels, James Michener's *The Bridges at Toko-ri* was probably the most popular as well as the best-written novel of the war. In it the author elaborates on the theme of the lonely warrior who is not convinced of his own contribution or that of the war itself. Perhaps, as some critics have suggested, the heroes in these works had too much time on their hands, and too much time to think. Nevertheless, many of the heroes of the Korean War novel show a distaste for what they were doing, the reward not offsetting the challenge anticipated. As the hero of James Michner's *The Bridges at Toko-ri* suggests, "Winning is not enough."

These novels of air and sea reflect the same concern expressed by the ground soldier: the lack of recognition and appreciation from the folks at home. Some authors write back into history the events they witnessed at the end of the war. This was the case in Walt Sheldon's *Tour of Duty* (1959), in which he not only condemned the poor homeland support but the lack of tactical and general strategy on the part of the leadership. The fact that the war appears to be forgotten manages to work its way into most of these novels of the war. The one major exception is Charles B. Flood's *A Distant Drum* (1957), which is able to avoid the issue while focusing on intra-personnel relationships.

One of the few distinguishing features found in the Korean War novel was the degree to which the characters had to deal with an advance in technological equipment and data. Many of the works provide a great deal of description and appreciation for the machines they drove and fought with. There is often a strong subplot that concerns the hero's love for his or her equipment and the technical abilities needed to operate it. The specialist takes on a new role that has often been used to separate the hero from the rest of the outfit.

The novels in question are less experimental and lack what literary critic Axelsson refers to as "imaginative embroidery." Part of the ongoing critique of Korean War novels is the choice of a reporting style best called "realism" that appears to have resulted for two reasons. One is the lack of information about the war or the military at the time, and thus a fear of drifting too far into speculation. But second, the Korean War in itself provided about all the surrealism and absurdity that could be assumed. Most likely influenced by nonfiction and what was identified as the new journalism, the Korean War novel tended to stick to this traditionally realistic framework: the autobiographical account "from boot camp to Pork Chop Hill" types; the occupation or garrison novel; the novel that "rises from innocence" to produce men; and the tale of the discovery of courage. But in most of these efforts, the authors had not yet been able to assemble a really intimate view of this unique war.

What is often a surprise to the critic is the degree to which Korean War novels are historically event-specific. That is, the degree to which they are surprisingly accurate. Descriptions of action are so well presented that it is often possible to locate the exact spot—the time and place—that the event occurred. Unlike novels of the world wars, the Korean War novel appears to be well-researched and recorded in such a manner to be historically correct. There is, as expected, some use of poetic license found or perhaps an adjustment to chronology to keep the story moving, but nevertheless surprising accurate. A second related fact is the degree to which authors admit that the selection and descriptions of characters are modeled, quite literally, after persons they knew or worked with.

In terms of plot, the focus it is surprisingly restrained. Of the nearly 120 novels listed in Axelsson as Korean War novels, the plots are pretty much limited to the invasion at Inchon, the retreat at Chosin Reservoir, MiGs over Korea, a particular hill battle, or brainwashing, in which are combined the twin fears of communism and the growing concern over psychic manipulation. One in four novels produced dealt with prisoners of war. In these stories it is clear that American novelists generally reflect the popularly held view that the behavior of the U.S. soldier in Korea left much to be desired from a patriotic and militarily professional standpoint.

In the more immediate sense, few of these novels move far away from "the small unit of misfits sent on an impossible mission" and who usually get lost. The characters of the squad consist of a pretty obvious collection: the natural leader, the religious nut, the rebel, the misfit, the old-timer, the sensitive author, the caring medic, and the boy from Brooklyn. Among these characters there are generally some racial concerns that, while not as desperate as many would suggest, still packed their share of troubles within a unit. In a surprising number of cases, racial prejudice is often presented as being overcome by the demands of front-line combat. Marvin Albert in his excellent book *All the Young Men* (1960), later made into a movie, spread the message of exposing prejudice and of the necessity of cooperation among other minorities as well: Puerto Ricans, Mexican, Jews, and even Orientals.

One thing that seems to be lacking in the literature is the emotional gap created by the transition of soldiers and sailors from "master at arms," the basic warrior who stood his or her ground, to the "managers of violence," representing the revolutionary alteration in the technology of war and challenging the very nature of the warrior himself. Little has been written about the soldier's awareness of his own less significant role.

Arne Axelsson, whose *Restrained Response* is obviously the finest study of Cold War literature that has been done, suggests a timeline that hovers over Korean War novels that mark market response as well as author's motivation. The initial author's response was the production of less than quality material, based on individual experience and elaborately embodied with personal involvement and often honor.

Many of the early works were written by experts with a great deal of insight into the nature of war, probably some experience, and were a cause to be celebrated. The second group consisted of those who came later and who represented observation as well as the experience that is most reflective of the enlisted man, the reservists. The third, and the authors who have been writing primarily from 1960s, are the professional writers who may or may not have had any experience. Rather they are equipped with the professional ability to research and to accommodate. One thing is very evident. The further away the book is written, the less historical and more emotional they become.

The respected literary critic Peter Jones believed that there was a shift in emphasis between World War II novels and those that took place in Korea. One such shift was that the enemy was no longer a disembodied mass of hated individuals, but rather the outcome of a political environment. At no point did there appear to be a person or a group with a mission. There was no real passionate need to write about the war, and thus few passionate appeals to understanding. None of the traditional "they killed my parents in a death camp" or the likes to provide motivation for extreme action.

The novels reflect concern that Americans in general, as well as American generals, acted on a policy of massive response, but made it difficult to deal with the measured reactions in combat that appeared to be more the realistic case. The Korean event, Jones suggested, displayed a new and unusual detachment from the larger issues and replaced the citizen-soldier of World War II with an imposed professional who did his job and little else. He was no longer passionately involved in the direction or the outcome at the time of his participation, and afterwards had no passionate need to justify his involvement. That is to say that the really reflective novel had not been written.

It is a great sadness that the military novels coming out of the Korea War have been so limited in quantity as well as in quality. It is sad that there are so few sources available to help the English-speaking readership recall and rekindle the events and the emotions of this significant period of American history. Unfortunately it is as true for the Korean War novel as for any war novel, that "for every *Farewell to Arms* there exists hundreds of pedestrian accounts of personal battles."[35]

Poetry

During World War I it has been estimated that more than a million poems were written, and a surprising number of these found their way into newspapers and magazine articles. During the war just about every man and a good many women used this genre because at this time poetry was the language of patriotism. And patriotism was the primary story being told. The war in all its romanticism, recognized as a holy struggle, was an event in which the fundamental trust became apparent. As Lewis Oglethorpe suggested, World War I was made for poetry. World War II produced far fewer poems, but they were better in quality and still classic enough to receive attention today.

The lack of poetry, good or bad, written from the period of the Korean War is hard to explain. The production just seems to stop. It accompanies a general lack of interest in either the writing or the reading of poetry, but it is more than that,[36] because a few years later the Vietnam War produced a good bit of poetry. During this time Americans had witnessed some serious changes both in the acceptance of poetry and the understanding of war.[37] Either way, the lack of such passion leaves a gap in the emotional data needed to individualize the impact of war, and the Korean War in particular.

By the time the war in Korea was being remembered a transition was taking place in the men and women who had been fighting a war they did not want to fight, in a place they did not want to be. It was perhaps the best of many awful options, and they were not inclined to consider it poetically. Even poetry was too much.

It may be too harsh a judgment, but one of the major sites for the evaluation of war poems, Poetry Soup.Com, lists the famous and well-loved poems from America's wars, but does not have a single entry for the Korean War. The page is blank.[38] So what can you say about a missing genre other than it is missing? If the few poems that have survived are a good measure of what may have been considered but never delivered, then there may be some merit at looking at them and drawing some primary conclusions.

It is not necessary to conduct too broad a survey to discover that Korean War poetry is effected by the "reordered time" approach that is often used to judge the historicity of poetry and prose. The historical content in military poetry that is written at the time of action is generally more reliable and historically accurate than those written afterwards. Often, the poem written much later contains a reflection of the memory as well as of the event. The same is true for novels written at the time.

What distinguishes most poetry that relates to or emerges from the Korean War is a lack of creative endeavor[39] that is self-predictive prophecies. The shortage of poetry makes it very difficult to sell the war as either a moral crusade or a political necessity. And the few who provide creative and imaginative analysis have not, as a general rule, seen the war as any sort of crusade. Nor do they believe that overall policy or intent has provided justification for the war. The response of the American poet surely reinforces General Ridgway's comment about it: "If any war that our country ever engaged in could have been called a forgotten war, this was it. The people in the States, I knew, were too preoccupied with the essentials of making a living to concern themselves in far away battles unless one of their immediate kin was involved."[40] By far the most recognized form of poetry is the nontraditional and the experimental form, designed in such a way that the form conveys part of the message. Much of what is available is written in free verse, which is to say, a lack of verse. Rhyme is generally found in sound rather than syllables. Most, as well, are written in the first person. Whether this further identifies the individual and isolated nature of the poetry is not obvious, but it does have the effect of making the reading more personal and thus less abstract or mystical, and therefore more provincial.

The available Korean War poetry appears to lack the sense of flow often expected in such works, and generally, for there are exceptions, are more blunt and negative in content. They express a sharp tone both in terms of language and attitude. The language, perhaps reflecting only the times, is far more plainspoken, full of harsh words and rampant with what among earlier poets might be identified as foul language. Many, but not to the extent Vietnam War poetry provided, are antiwar but tend to reflect criticism of the conditions of this particular situation (Korea), but not of war itself, as is found in so much World War I verse.

Related, but still different, many suggest a valiant tone with no underlying mantra, that is little unusual word choice. The value of literature, in this case, is that it helps us understand what has happened. Often it is in counterpoint to stories told by the general population. Self-reflective of both the warrior and the war, they provide a new generation of ideological language in which to talk about post-traumatic memory, historical references, and thematic storytelling. But all involved were aware that no interpretation will erase the damage that had been done.

Essays

Under more normal circumstances, it would be expected that the essay would have the most to say about the events of the war and the culture's response. The essay is designed to isolate a topic and to make a point in a short and enjoyable fashion. It is at one time unique in its ability to focus and clear in the presentation of the idea. While generally personal in tone, even subtly humorous, the essay addresses serious topics. Generally short, often written quickly and with a sense of serendipity, the essay is famous for drawing the public attention to those things they appear to have forgotten. From Tom Paine's call to revolution to Paul Fussell's "Thank God for the Atom Bomb," the essay has been one of America's great tools for cultural communication.

The essay has become less popular over the last few decades. In many respects the continued existence of such magazines as *The New Yorker, Atlantic,* and *Smithsonian,* to name a few, have kept the essay alive—and published some of the finest and most insightful comments. What is still being published reflects an interest in current events and attitudes, either explaining them, challenging them, or comparing them to the nation's tradition. There is, however, little analysis of the Korean War, and in fact even very little comment concerning the event or its legacy. An essay is basically a think piece, a musing about what has happened or what something means, even the search for some way to say what the essayist has interpreted. But, apparently, the war is not a concern among those who might provide us such insights. The major "intellectual" journals still provide us with commentary on just about everything from the rebirth of sweet potatoes to global warming; but this long-ignored war has not sparked these imaginations. There is no American equivalent of the Chinese essayist Wei Wei's "Who are the Most Beloved People."

Sounds

No stretch of the imagination is remarkable enough to suggest that there were any memorable Korean War songs. As far as can be determined, there has been no classical music created in commemoration of the Korean War, and much of that identified as popular music has mercifully been forgotten. Just about the best that can be said about the musical response to the Korean War is that it served as a transition between the strong patriotism and sacrifice reflected in the popular music of World War II and the heavy protest melodies of the Vietnam War.

Classical music, as it is generally identified, is nearly nonexistent in its response to Korea. There are very few things that get no response when called up on the Internet, but classical music in honor of the Korean War is one of them. Perhaps there has not been enough time, but in the nearly three-quarters of a century, few American composers have put the passion of this war into music. Nothing of the caliber of Tchaikovsky's *1812 Overture* or Dmitri Shostakovich's Symphony #7 (*Leningrad*) has yet appeared, and the future possibility of such a work is severely limited. There is little available on the lists of sheet music for formal choirs. Few musicals have been produced. There are few topics that are not included in the lists of sheet music for formal choirs, but Korea is one of them. Some classical music has been composed in other countries and performed here, but none of our own.

If you look, you will discover a modest but somewhat predictable appearance of popular music that came out of the war. Those that became available were very specifically directed toward the Korean War, including little of the collateral effects of war. In the main they tend to express the same themes as other soldiers' songs: patriotism, faith, hope, courage, pain, and loneliness. They generally make the distinction between identifying front-line topics, and the opposing home front, as well as changes that have occurred in the lives of those participating.

These songs are few in number and their distribution was fairly limited. Most are unavailable today other than in archives, and even these are scarce. None of the music emerging out of Korea came even close to the popularity level of Fats Domino's "Ain't That a Shame," Patti Page's "Tennessee Waltz," Nat King Cole's "Too Young," or Ray Charles's "I Got a Woman." Usually a performer would include one song about the war on a record or during a show, but none emerged like "Over There," or "Coming in on a Wing and a Prayer," that automatically identified the song with the war.

Patriotism was an obvious theme, but in the main it was more generalized; that is, more of the "God Bless America" sentiments in which the singer seeks God's help in the success of the conflict, and fewer about what was happening in Korea. Little was written about specific locations or battles. The "Stars and Stripes," the common cause, the love of freedom, all appear in one form or the other, but those mentioning patriotism never seem to have caught on as well as songs based on emotional topics.

Jimmie Osborne released his "The Voice of Free America" in which he supports America's Cold War position. Some few were written about the use, or possible use, of nuclear weapons. The most popular of these was when Jackie Doll and his Pickled Peppers Band came out with "When They Drop the Atom Bomb."

Some of the songs tried to deal with what the author believed was on the soldier's mind day by day. "Rotation Blues" by Stuart Powell is a poignant song that recounts the months of collecting enough rotation points to go home. "The Honey Pots in Korea Started Smelling" invokes some understanding of the conditions under which these men fought. While there were some occasions in which an individual was honored with a song, they were very few. Heroics were not really as popular in Korea as they had been in the European war, and there were fewer individuals to be sought out; no Sergeant York or Audie Murphy on which to build a legend. General Douglas MacArthur was a special case; several songs appeared about the general and most were positive. Gene Autry sang "Old Soldiers Never Die"; however, few of these songs mention events in Korea, but rather sang his praises for his exploits during World War II and the Philippines.

Faith, or lack of it, was a familiar topic, more so at home than abroad. As expected, many turned to religion for guidance and hope, and it made sense that songs would appear to validate these feelings. One of the earliest songs to come out of the war was Jimmie Osborne's "God Please Protect America." It first appeared shortly after the outbreak of war and highlighted the need for spiritual direction in a dire time. Many of the songs available acknowledge the need of divine protection.

A good many songs appear that were apparently written to affirm, or maybe recall, a strong faith in God that would save the American people from disaster and individual soldiers from harm. There were as well prayers for peace that tended to appear more toward the end of the war and after the armistice. Getting carried away with the first signs of victory, several works appeared to celebrate the event long before it existed. These included Osborne's "Thank God for Victory in Korea."

The songs also highlighted those events that disheartened the soldier. Top among these was the loss of the girl back home, the news of which was delivered by an unexpected "Dear John" letter. The general concern was expressed in "The Korean Blues" about a soldier wondering who was sleeping in his bed at home. The most popular song on this subject was "A Dear John Letter," recorded in May 1953, which remained on the country music charts for six weeks. Jean Shepherd's song tells of a soldier who received a letter from his girl saying she had fallen in love with his brother.[41]

Much darkness is recounted in music that deals with those missing in action, with the pain of getting the KIA telegram, the sibling loss, the return of an unfinished diary, the loss of a young father. There were, of course, songs designed to recall the emotions of the final sacrifice. Carl Sauseman's "A White Cross Marks your Grave" is one of the better of these highly emotional productions.

In general the songs are distinctively naive and talk about the war in large abstractions with little interest in, or ability to, recall the real cost of combat. The then-famous cowboy star Gene Autry joined with Wesey Tuttle and Ernest Tubbs to provide versions of "A Heartsick Soldier on Heartbreak Ridge." Eldon Britt's "Korean Mud" tells the story of a soldier who dies because blood plasma did not get to him in time. The same theme of loss in vain is central to "The Unknown Soldier," in which the composer suggests he will be forever haunted by the spirits of those allowed to die, and to die in vain. The underevaluated death was considered a dishonor.

Following the armistice, Sister Rosetta Tharperr released "There's Peace in Korea," which was well received for a short time. She followed it up by several songs in memory of the dead. Most of the Korean War songs were only as popular as the artist, and there were rarely many renditions. None seemed to join the classics from previous wars.

In time the jingoism of earlier songs give way to the sadness and the pain of separation. The quick patriotism expressed in time is softened by concerns of faith and affirmations. The plight of the POW almost never appears in song and was not the topic of consideration that it has been in other culture memories. However, "The Red Deck of Cards" reaffirms communist propaganda and warns of the danger returning home with a good many of our soldiers.

The prime emotional pain appears to be separation, as in "Korea Here We Come," which accounts the experience of being recalled into service. Wilif Carter's "Good-bye Maria, I'm off to Korea," talks about the moment of leaving, while Sonney Osbourne laments the loss of brothers and the general evils of battle in "A Brother in Korea."

A fair number of songs written for and popular during World War I were transferred over to World War II and were adopted with that war. The words and attitudes did not seem out of place in the later war. In Korea, however, there was little cross-over and less longevity. It is hard to imagine a Korean version of "Praise the Lord and Pass the Ammunition."

Yet peace came quickly to the music world, and most of these songs were off the charts and out of the juke boxes within a few weeks. Like so many other things that were happening, the nature of music was changing as well as the tastes of those in the market. There was no continuing interest. Today a quick look at the nostalgia section of the music catalogues will provide access to songs of World War I or II. You can even get German marching songs recorded in 1914. But no collection of songs from the Korean War period.

Looking back, one wonders about the number and intensity of anti-war songs. Those raised with Joan Baez and the whole genre of protest songs of the '60s and '70s will wonder at this, but there was almost no protest against war in general and only one or two against Korea. As noted elsewhere, the America of the 1950s tended to be far more apathetic. But as might be expected, the famed Woody Guthrie recorded his protest in "I've Got to Know."

In terms of musical remembrances, Korea did not inspire the sort of music that lasts, as for example the many songs of World War I that are still sung today. Why? Perhaps it is just one more example of the lack of intensity with which Americans viewed the event.

Sights

The sad role of the musical remembrance is generally duplicated by the lack of graphic works depicting the war. During World Wars I and II, and even Vietnam and post–Vietnam wars, the military units have had assigned combat artists to record the war in original drawings. In Korea, however, the army did not have any such persons identified. They finally decided to put six painters into combat units to record the action in drawing and paintings. Much of the output is magnificent, but there is not a great deal of it. What is more, the lack of artists in the units means that later talents would be less likely to consider the combat drawing as a significant output. Most units had combat photographers, but a surprisingly high percentage of the photos they took were of events and dignitaries.[42]

Most of the artists involved were already associated with commercial magazines and the record of their postwar creations is limited. But there is very little military art of the period available. A few remarkable photographs were identified; certainly David Duncan's *Give me tomorrow*, a photo of an infantryman in Korea will always be remembered. But the graphic side of the press suffered somewhat from the limited coverage that the written press experienced. Paintings are available and they and drawings and etchings have found their way into the market or the gallery. But only one or two are of the quality of Pablo Picasso, whose 1951 painting *Massacre in Korea* stands as high criticism of American participation in the Korean War.[43]

The same is true of free-standing sculpture, with the most significant statues perhaps being the statues of the Korean War Veterans Memorial in Washington, D.C. Some of the local memorials have produced a few works in stone and metal. But little is of the quality found in Yul-san Liem's *Bridge of Return*, a highly symbolic rendering of the bridge over which the POW returned home. Perhaps the best-known piece of sculpture from the war is that of Staff Sergeant Reckless (1948–1968), a well-known Marine supply mule who was commemorated at the National Marine Corps Museum in Quantico, Virginia, in July 2013.

Memorials and Monuments

The creation of a museum dedicated to the Korean War has become something of a joke among veterans. Most of the efforts have proven unsuccessful, and yet the fundraising continues. There are also a few storefront collections, usually unincorporated, and a somewhat obscure unit known as a nationally designated Museum of the Korean War. Just what this is and who it represents is unclear, as is where it is located.

A dedicated museum, if there were a demand for it, would be difficult to provide anyway. Such a collection is almost superfluous for the simple reason that the vast majority of artifacts that would be collected—uniforms, weapons, communications equipment, and personal items—would be little different from those on display in World War II museums. Few items would be available to tell a different story, since the different story of this war is primarily one of attitude, not artifact. But perhaps there is enough available if one could locate unique items as propaganda efforts, electronic experiments, jets, helicopters, enemy artifacts, MASH units, and the effects of personnel made famous by the war.

A good number of the better museums in this country were created as private collections or were established as part of the agenda of someone of wealth who had a particular interest in the items being displayed. So far no such person has emerged to support a Korean project. It is too bad that neither the government nor private enterprise has seen the need for a museum dedicated to the Korean War. Why? Because the museum holds in trust the heart of the culture for all future generations to witness. The display—hands-on history, it is often called—is a basic source of reference for a culture seeking to acknowledge and celebrate its past. While the displays are important, and need to be created with great sensitivity and insight, it is the other 75 percent of the material patiently waiting in storage for its display that is important. To paraphrase the more famous statement, materials also serve that just wait until their story needs to be told.

Once more the failure to put such museum together, the tendency to lump all remaining artifacts with World War II, the lack of any interest in acknowledging the war as a cultural step in our development, all weaken the impact of those events on future generations as well as denying the people involved the only voice they have left.

The most important item in a museum is its director, who, whether he intends to or not, will alter the history of the war by the placement of the artifacts. Basic to such displays is the often misunderstood definition of the artifact. Is a chair taken from Appomattox in which General Lee sat and surrendered the Army of Northern Virginia significant because Lee sat in it, or because it reflects the period in which Lee was surrendering? "Lincoln Slept Here," we were told in our afternoon visit to Springfield, Illinois. Was that important because it displayed a common bed of an important era of history, or because a later-to-be-great man rested his bones on it? Are the grenades of Korea important, or only the grenade carried by Matthew Ridgway? For the curator, terms like significant, important, reflective, or even functional, take on new roles.[44]

Museums are a society's reflection of commitment. They are symbols of what is important and displays of what has survived. Duration, on the other hand, is a key factor in the extent of our commitment. It is in the duration of involvement that the depth of a nation's commitment is made; and in the duration of commitment that the seriousness is determined. So far duration seems to be questionable. The long-term investment, so indicative of real commitment, is lacking in many aspects relating to the memory. Perhaps none is so obvious as the limited care of the Korean Veterans War Memorial.

Persons studying such things as war memorials indicate that they are primarily reflective of one of two questions: one, did we win or lose; and two, was it necessary or unnecessary? The memorials also tend to reflect much of the mood of the society, not when the event took place, but when the commemoration was designed. Thus the memorial is created to remember the memory, not necessarily the event, in mind.

Following the Revolutionary War there was very little attention paid to remembering either the event or those who fought it. Such memories gained popularity in the following century. After the Civil War, however, the events effected so many people and were so based on deep ideological causes, that the commemoration was exaggerated. With both sides respecting the beliefs of the other, as well as the need to grieve, thousands of memorials were created. Because of the geographical nature of the "cause for war," they tend to reflect places, often dedicated to the men of a given town or a county or state unit. Cemeteries reflecting each side began to appear as memorials.

While victory was apparent, necessity was not, and the Mexican War, like the Spanish-American War, were primarily void of monuments. It was not until after America's involvement in World War I that more monuments appeared, both in the United States and abroad. The memorials tended to celebrate units and the battles in which they fought. Following World War II the inclination was to memorialize places rather than units. Reflecting the then common belief that the war was fought to free people, the nation tended to relate the event to the people, by naming memorial buildings, community service centers, plazas, parks, and formal gardens after them. But there were very few of the more traditional statues, Iwo Jima being the exception.

Of that series of wars that American clearly did not win, or the fighting of which was considered unnecessary, there are few memorials in the United States. Little can be found to emblaze Perry's victory on Lake Erie, or Andrew Jackson at New Orleans.[45]

The fact that the Korean War came out negative to both essential questions makes it somewhat easier to understand why memorials were slow to appear and hard to find. Very few were proposed or built during the years following the war. Those that were created tended to hold up the minorities involved and, reflecting the mood of the nation, introduced the "politically correct" memorial. However, as the 1980s approached, the veterans began to come alive to their service and began to agitate local communities for memorials. It worked, and many were created. However, in almost every case it was the veteran and not the community that raised the money and saw to the erection of the work. Today many states and quite a few counties have memorials, some tucked away in an isolated park and some on urban display in the larger cities. A large number are geographical and personnel oriented: "Dedicated to the men of Howard County who served in the Korean War."

After years of haggling, political juggling, false starts, committee competition, fundraising failures, congressional opposition and downright lack of political interest, the long-awaited memorial to the Korean War Veteran was finally dedicated by President Bill Clinton. The monument was only symbolically built by the American people. The prime motivation and actual costs of constructions came mainly from veterans groups and private companies, including decisive amounts provided by corporations in the Republic of (South) Korea—the Korean Motor Company primarily. At the moment, the care and maintenance of the memorial is not well funded, nor is there any agency whose responsibility it is to keep it clean and in repair. The wall of remembrance was added only when a private donor agreed to pay the costs. Now, in 2016, it is badly in need of repair and its few supporters are desperately trying to locate funds. Whatever it meant in that brief moment in time when events came together and allowed it to be built, it is now suffering from the limitation of man's memory.

It is important to note that there is a specter hovering about our past. And it is expanding deeper and deeper into America's depositories of its history. This specter, like so many dangers, is basically misunderstood and generally undetected. It is the result of a threefold interaction of events. One is the hard fact that more and more of our state and national museums are funded by benefactors who make controlling the agenda the basis of the gift. Second is the wide availability of digital imagery and technology craftsmanship that can create "historical references" that are not artifacts, but rather mental stimulants that represent something that did not exist. The third is the increasing support for the idea that America's strength lies in a free and self-identifying capitalism.

These museums, therefore, represent a created past rather than a discovered one. They represent war as a tool of that capitalism in a way that is not a totally honest reflection of American wars, and especially not the Korean War. We are experiencing the emergence of beautifully designed and well-crafted museums that call up a memory that does not necessarily reflect the traditions and agenda of the American people. Rather, they are designed to convey a structure of memorials that increasingly espouse the stages of neoliberalism and national militarism.[46]

The aim of these endeavors is to educate the American people about its wars, to acknowledge the lives of those who made the final sacrifice for the good of the nation, and to tie the patriotism of war and national conviction to the creation and maintenance of an elite military class and the expansion the private sector into area previously in the hands of the government. Perhaps the most ambitious and highly successful role model for this effort is the newly completed Hall of Military History, dedicated on Veterans Day, 2009, in Washington, D.C. The cash for the construction of this hall that bears his name came as a gift of eighty million dollars from real estate giant Kenneth Behring, who, as a result, has a great deal to say about what is in it and how it is displayed.

The museum and its sponsor have been successful in making the institution a role model for a trend that is reprogramming the past in an effort to alter the view of the future. It does this by creating a connection between what the image maker wants you to remember and what you are inclined to forget. The result is a museum that recalls that which never happened in an effort to support that which has not yet happened.

When you find an artifact at the historic site and do not display it, you have lost a significant impact on the larger event. But when you create an artifact that was not there (a poster, photo image, animated reactions, reproductions), you not only alter the larger image, you inject the present into a part of the past. And in so doing, you weaken the verification of understanding. If you find a pipe-hatchet from a minor Sioux tribe at the Big Horn and ignore it, you may be failing to identify all the tribes involved. But when you create the photo of a manufactured metal pipe-hatchet, of the kind sold to the Indians by the Eastern industrial complex, you have injected commercial America into an unwelcoming past. It makes a good display, and it is not necessarily wrong, but it is deceptive.[47]

The new message is one that glorifies war in such a manner to convey the message that privatizing the American economy, and aggrandizing the army as its protector, is told in part by the messenger. This is the result of a totally independent hands-on control of public displays based on images that have been created, not uncovered.

The association of this museum with the Smithsonian Institution lends an authentic image to the items on display. Displays that are made suspicious by the nature of privatization are by definition a discredit to any objectivity. While true, it may not matter all that much, since artifacts preserved tend to be less relics of wars and more and more commodities reflecting the commercial character of the nation equipping the military. This is not because there are no artifacts to display, but rather to avoid whatever explanation the artifact required, and to make room for a cinematic illustration of a war that reflects novel forms of nationalism coming into focus in the age of neoliberals. These displays, identified by Marita Sturken, professor of communications, as "technologies of memory," are designed to introduce national subjects into past events by the insertion of a cultural memory.

This is not some subtle, hidden agenda clandestinely formulated by diabolical persons. The effort is wide open. A comment by Brent D. Glass, the director of the project in Washington, D.C., says it all pretty clearly: "The displays extend far beyond a survey of battles. They also describe the relationship between military conflict and American political leadership, social values, technological innovation and personal sacrifice."[48]

More specifically, the display on the Korean War is not so much to proclaim its meaning in the midst of the Cold War but rather to downplay—almost dismiss—it as a contribution to the nation.[49] It is located in a small room at one end of the long and elaborate Cold War exhibit, where the location, the size, and the low insensitivity of the Korean display suggest the curators felt that the war had little social, economic, or political significance.[50] There is no doubt that the curators at least considered it a proxy war fought out of the natural distrust of two superpowers, but little else. On arrival at the room, after working through the massive exhibits of World War II and 9/11, the visitor will discover it is one of the only rooms that lacks a soundtrack. Rather, the guest listens to the muted music and mumbled voices from a dozen other displays. Unlike the carefully crafted displays of 9/11, the Korean display seems haphazard, and if there is any organization apparent, it is in the distinction between the divided nature of Korea as a political and economic bloc, and the hardship of soldiers stationed there.

There is, among other absences, no discrete or self-contained history of the event, but the story (not the history) is rather forcefully inserted into the larger Cold War that theoretically is a better representation of the event. As is true of so many "memories" of the events in Korea, the highly costly war is presented as a feeble echo of the Second World War and a partial prefiguring of the Vietnam War. Once again, "the shrimp caught between whales."

The walk-through experience reminds many of Douglas Sirk's melodramatic war film *Battle Hymn* (1959), the creation of which is one of most self-flattering stories that Americans have been able to make up about themselves. The film is an elaborate effort to provide moral justification for their devastating intervention into the Korean War. In it the mythmaker manages to depict American servicemen as protecting and saving the Asian orphans rather, than as was the case, being the creator of the problem.

Taking the whole experience as an event in itself, it mineralizes the characterization of war, making it a tool not only of American policy, but American economics. The ideological assumption that drove the nation for years—the fear of communism—is highly muted. It belittles the Korean War experience by presenting it in much the same category as the Trail of Tears or the War of 1812. But while these are unfortunate, they are not the danger. The danger is that the crafting of digital production in order to tell the story forgoes the need for justification of the artifact, and allows the independent producers (money sources) to fashion a past in support of a present and future they wish to see.

IX

Brainwashed, Yes,
but Who?

May you never forget what is worth remembering nor ever remember what is best forgotten.—Irish Blessing

Yes, there was brainwashing going on, but the question is who was doing it, and to whom was it being done? The idea, popular from its first suggestion, has always held a fascination for the American people and a good many still believe that the communists successfully brainwashed many United States soldiers. This unfortunate idea, first coined by Edward Hunter in *New Leader Magazine* in 1951, is greatly responsible for giving the communists credit for what they did not accomplish, and for ignoring much of what we should have learned about those sent to fight the war. Perhaps seeking some excuse for the poor outcome, both the press and the military overdid the "brainwashing" idea which, unfortunately became popularized by such novels and films as *The Manchurian Candidate*.

One might expect that the signing of the armistice would bring an end to the war's influence and the beginning of healing. That time would have made our view of the events more universal and the meaning more acceptable. But that has not been the case. Americans are inclined to think of the term armistice as they remember it from World War I: as a first step victory and the beginning of a new era. Nothing was settled in Korea. The line in the sand is more deeply drawn each year. Hardly a week passes that something reminds us that the war is still going on. Years ago when America was stuck in Vietnam, Senator J. William Fulbright used to say, "Why not just tell everyone that we won, and come home?" When is the last time the United States actually won a war? How long has it been since we just "came home"? We are not even sure these days that we could identify what a victory consisted of, what it would look like. Perhaps withdrawal, inactivity, isolation may be the long-sought "substitute for victory" that was chased. Without full knowledge of our expectations, it is perhaps far easier to simply leave a few thousand troops behind and go about our other business, saying no more about it.

Allowed to remain unchallenged, the great myths of this war have simply been revamped to support the prejudices that we have already formed. The war and its legends simply support the attitudes and expectations that we have mistakenly drawn, casting a distorted vision on the nation's history. The impartial judge observing from some mythical neutrality might look down upon us and say that the history of warfare since the end of the Korean War is all the proof that we need that the nation learned little if anything from it. It might well be said that Americans have forgotten about Korea because it was experienced at such low intensity that it did not attach itself to, and thus properly alter, the long-term memory of our nation or our civilization.

Brainwashing requires far more focus than does propaganda, and while they may well have the same results, it was the latter that explained the vast array of vague misconceptions and shadowy assumptions held by the American people about the war and the peace. The ensuing confusion and misdirection still appear within the memories of veterans, in the accounts of old-timers, and more unfortunately in schoolbook texts, essays, commentaries, dissertations and analysis.

Surrogate Victory

Contrary to the recent remarks of President Obama, the war in Korea was not a victory. But it did have its moments of success. Political maneuvering and spin doctors have done a pretty good job of turning the loss in Korea into enough of a victory that we can put it in the win column. One source of this "historical correction" has been the change of focus from victory as achieved by the enemy's surrender, and victory as was acknowledged by the return of all the POWs. It has been the success of a surrogate victory.

The Kansas State Board of Education recently responded to its students' failing the standard tests by suggesting if they can't pass the test we give them, then let's give them a test they can pass. Likewise, the goal of the Korean War appeared to be increasingly unwinnable, and so the policy makers changed the look of victory. We were no longer demanding the reunification or the de-socialization of Korea; we were seeking the return of all our prisoners.

The fact that we did not achieve an unconditional surrender from the communists most certainly plays a large role in the amnesia overtaking America. But there was more to it than the failure to live up to the Jacksonian demands of military morality. It was more than military loss. The line had been drawn and it was believed. To win is essential, to lose sometimes a necessary reality, but to abandon a fight with an evil nation is immoral. It is the lack of morality that most Americans want to forget. The nation lied to its people about its causes, its motivations, and its responsibilities. Whether the nation was lying to itself is hard to know. When success became unobtainable, at least not at the anticipated costs, the administration struggled to identify the return of prisoners as the mark of victory.

In the mind of the Truman administration, the voluntary repatriation of prisoners became a surrogate for a conclusion. Fairly quietly and without a lot of justification, the battle cry went out. There would be no negotiated agreement on the end of the war until the communists agreed to voluntary repatriation. We took a firm stand; we would listen to no compromise. And, while the Chinese fought and screamed that they would do no such thing, the discussion changed and the expectations weakened and died. Yet, in time, the communists accepted the totally untraditional and antihistorical point of view of President Truman, and agreed to repatriate the POWs.[1] But, then, it really didn't have that effect and the administration knew it.

In time the negotiations came to an end; an end to both our discussions of the war and to negotiations of all POWs. The inability to arrive at any reasonable solution to anything pretty well acknowledged that no negotiations were taking place, and gloom took over the talks. The disinclination to deal with the unresolved problems became as much an issue in need of settlement as did any blocks to compromise. The harshness of positions on both sides of the DMZ shows little signs of letting up. The discussions were only distantly related to the immediacy of the war.

Fought by the United States

However vague is the American memory of the Korean War, one thing is certain, and that is that the war was fought by Americans. The United Nations takes a minor or nonexistent role. Not only did numerous other nations use their positions in the United Nations to put forth and approve the necessary resolutions of involvement, but a good number of nations sent men and women to fight. Any wide understanding or appreciation for the nearly fifty other nations involved in the war is nearly forgotten. In its usual lumbering and argumentative manner, the UN nevertheless committed its member nations to aid the Republic of Korea (South). But the United Nations is less and less a part of the memory, and its contributions of fighting men and equipment, medical corps and ambulance units, is rarely part of the discussion.

The United States provided men and equipment, but they did not provide it all. The largest contributor to the war, and the most easily forgotten, were the men and women of the Republic of Korea (South) Army, Navy, and Marines. The bulk of the fighting and the majority of the dying involved the ROKA. The exact number called into service is hard to determine since much of their force consisted of *ad hoc* commands or were assimilated into other military units. But well over 600,000 South Korean troops were involved one time or another. The failure to acknowledge this is partly Western (American) elitism, and partly a lack of regard for the Korean people. But no matter how you color the situation, these primarily forgotten people were the mainstay.

The focus of most studies directed toward Asia are concerned with China or Japan. Only rarely and most recently has interest in either of the Koreas been high. For many years, the Korean language was not taught in the United States. There were few cultural centers for understanding the people of Korea, and few persons in America could claim to know, or even know of, a Korean family. There was nothing in the American past that would have aided in the negotiations.

Few official histories of the South Korean involvement are available.[2] When war broke out, the ROKA was in desperate need of assistance, and in July of 1950 Congress passed the Deficiency Appropriations Act in order to provide immediate need. In an act of military unity, President Rhee, on 14 July 1950, placed all his troops under the command of General MacArthur. After that, distinctions between participation and accomplishment was not always clear. Eighth Army considered themselves a single fighting force and the ROKA was openly assigned as affiliates rather than full partners. Speaking today, most veterans of the period looked down on the ROKA, and those who were not there are slow to acknowledge the costly role they played.

But it wasn't just ROKA; many others fought and died side-by-side with the American forces. George M. Elsey, the White House advisor, wrote in July 1950 that the Allied reaction to Truman's decision to intervene in Korea was highly favorable and accumulated considerable support. It was not without question, but most nations seemed to reflect the view of the French Foreign Minister Robert Schuman, that Truman's response was the only proper one available. Even nations like Syria, Jordan and Iraq managed to provide vaguely worded documents of support, but Egypt could not manage to do even that. However, while slow to act and not overly generous, more than forty nations contributed to the effort within the next few months.[3]

Few Americans are aware of the highly significant contribution provided by the British Commonwealth,[4] from the first days of the war. Overshadowed by Vietnam, the role of the French in the early weeks of the war has gone unnoticed. Dozens of other nations, many small and with limited forces themselves, fought even if only symbolically in order to provide a united force.

Official histories have made little effort to acknowledge these contributions and to recognize how much the United States needed them. Such a failure to understand weakens the role of the United Nations and downgrades the powerful influence of combined allies focused on the same cause. It's insulting as well to the men and women who fought, and the many who died, in that joint effort.

There was a great deal of prejudice shown the Korean people, the carryover term gook being used to describe these less-than-human creatures. While most Americans do not think of North Korea much at all, when they do there is a prejudice against them in this country, especially by the veterans. Men who brought home "war brides" found the government a lot less than sympathetic, and the home town folks antagonistic and without understanding. Unlike that extended to the war brides of World War II, the American greeting was not as welcoming. The best estimate is that of the 6,423 Korean women who came to the United States as war brides, some 80 percent of their marriages resulted in divorce. Little has been done to compensate for the Kijoch'on, the military camptowns where Korean women were forced to provide sexual services to the military of several nations.[5] The military support of Rhee's vicious crackdown and massacre of his ideological enemies remains a festering discomfort in both Koreas. The people in the North do not understand the extremes of warfare leveled against them, particularly the necessity of carpet bombing, and they keep the memory of the war alive through ongoing propaganda.

Much has been written about the role of the United Nations in both the Korean War and the Cold War. It is only necessary to remark on a corollary to the above myth, which is that the war was fought and won by the United Nations. This is probably not true either. It was the first war fought under the flag of the United Nations, but it was not a war fought by the United Nations. The war in Korea was fought by the men and women of two dozen nations, but it was fought as an American war.

Even the United Nations was aware of the difficulties of fighting a war by committee, and so the body requested that the United States accept the role as "executive agent" for implementing the United Nations resolution. In response Truman named General Douglas MacArthur as commander in chief for all United Nations forces. The difficulties created by such an organization are hard to imagine. The various nations involved brought with them their political baggage and subtle agendas, aggravated by the fact they did not speak a common language, use common equipment, or fight by the same tactics. The problems created by logistics, as well as by politics, meant that some nations that offered aid were refused.

Likewise, in going to war in the name and under the flag of the United Nations, Truman's maneuvering gave credence to American policy. At the same time, it helped save the UN from the sort of crisis that destroyed the League of Nations, by giving it a cause, and one that it could address. Whether the UN has worked out for good or ill is another debate better argued on other issues, but one fact is clear. It has played a significant role in world politics.

The DMZ: Polite and Friendly

It is hard to believe that some Americans consider the Demilitarized Zone (DMZ) a tourist spot. But they do; coming to a place advertised by travel agents as "The World's Most Dangerous Border," they gleefully head for a piece of land so hostile they must sign a waiver that if they are killed or wounded, the South Korean government will not be held responsible. It seems a little much. The Demilitarized Zone has become a showcase whose luster belies the seriousness of the situation. What was originally a checkpoint for passage between the two nations has become a busy, rambling compound that maintains a public face of compromise and consideration, but which provides little of either. President Bill Clinton, visiting in 1993, declared it "the scariest place on earth."

Today, the point of union at which these two halves of the divided nation come together is, predictably, the most heavily armed border on the face of the earth. This plot of land 155 miles long and 2.5 miles wide is in a constant state of alert and backed up by massive firepower. The line roughly follows the 38th parallel, with the western tip crossing the South and the eastern tip breaching the North. The significant markers are at the North Limit Line and the Demarcation Line. The only point at which you can cross over the Demarcation Line and stand in North Korea is at the Military Armistice Commission Conference Room in the joint Security Area. The other points at which the nation is divided are marked by a series of posts, and crossing this line is considered a violation of the armistice. The outer limits of both sides have been marked with concertina, a spiraled barbed wire, and guarded by sets of towers in which machine guns face the enemy.

The scene is surrealistic, more like a movie stage than the hotspot of a lingering Cold War. Underneath the Zone are a series of four very sophisticated tunnels built by the North Koreans as invasion routes to the South. With the capacity to drive a tank through them, they stand ready, if forever monitored by the United Nations.

The broadcasting of propaganda materials across the line to harass each other was discontinued in 2015, though it sometimes returns briefly. Balloons carrying propaganda are often released over the line. On occasion the North Korean government allows citizens to approach and shout to their southern neighbors. Once in a while, usually dependent on the mood of the North Korean Great Leader, citizens are allow to move across between gates on Highway #1 to spend a few hours with their families. Within the Zone there are two legal villages that predate the war: Kijong dong and Sung. They are governed by the United

Nations command and the area is used primarily for farming. The villagers, descendants of the early settlers, must be on the land 227 days a year in order to keep their permission. Life there is surprisingly neutral, and in many respects its isolation has allowed it to become a wildlife sanctuary where animals from both sides can enjoy the situation.

The buildings on the compound house the military whose job it is to patrol the zone. Offices, medical facilities, intelligence gathering as well as the camp headquarters for the army commands, have headquarters. At the meeting place handsome, well-dressed soldiers of the Democratic People's Republic of Korea and the Republic of Korea, and/or the United States, stand tall, trying to appear harsh and tough as all kinds of tourists wander about staring at them. If lucky, you can see the changing guard march in and out in sync.

The optimistic expectation that daily discussions at the DMZ would allow our representatives to work out the immediate or existing problems did not last beyond the first day of confrontation. The sessions quickly turned into the exchange of complaints about violations and threats of retaliation. There is little to no negotiation going on. The anticipated talks designed to smooth the path to peace have become little other than a ritual where reason, cooperation and compromise have long since been ruled out of order.

Every few months there is some sort of incident, like the Ax Murder in which the two sides clashed over the cutting down of a tree, but with the exception of the Second Korean War it has remained fairly stable despite the threats and yelling.

In a fashion, and mimicking their coverage of the war, the American press has shown little inclination to report events along the Zone. Daily incidents leading to the death of one or two soldiers is not considered as front-page material, and even such highly significant periods known as the Second Korean War (1966–1969) received little attention. Granted, coverage of the Vietnam War was paramount at the time, but the acts of terrorism, guerrilla fighting, sabotage, and deaths of American soldiers deserved more attention. Even the loss of the USS *Pueblo*, with all its violations of international law and the armistice agreement, was treated lightly.[6]

The situation is formal, like the changing of the guard at Buckingham Palace. But it s a façade. This is a dangerous place where Americans, and Koreans North and South, continue to die on a regular basis. Unlike the American experience in Japan following the surrender, time has healed nothing. The conflict has only deepened, leaving both nations to deal with the lasting effects of the situation. The lack of resolution and "the conflict and the continuing political antagonism between the two sides has made it impossible for all parties to grasp their understanding of the war in an open, honest examination of the record from all sides."[7]

Korean War Created the Red Scare

It is hard for Americans to remember the Red Scare and how it altered this nation. Like the Great Depression, it comes up once in awhile and is used as an example of the irresponsible abuse of civil rights. It was more than just an event, and certainly had its roots deep in America's fear of socialism. Starting early and based on misinterpretations of the Russian Revolution, it was reflected in the emergence of workers' riots in the 1920s and the growing membership in the International Workers Party. The haunting specter of the "great communist conspiracy" was a powerful influence in this country, but it was not the product of the United States' intervention in Korea in 1950.

During the final years of World War I, as the American soldier fought the Hun, there was concern over the lack of patriotism. George Creel, chairman of the Office of Public Information, waged a campaign to identify those with less than patriotic leaning—the draft dodgers, socialists, dissenters, unionists—as communists, and it became the buzzword for treachery. The nation was hardly communistic, but was nevertheless showing signs of response to the ideals expressed in the worker' revolt. These "rebellions," packaged in symbolic activities as the May Day (May 1) parades, celebrated the success of the Communist Party in Russia. There was some terrorism and riots as striking workers got out of hand, and the blame was directed to the antichrist: the communists.

But for reasons the sociologists have not well explained, the movement stopped. Americans went about their daily lives, and there was less and less concern over ideological counterpoints. Then within a decade, the great fear reappeared as the growth of international communism led to an increase in American membership, though at no time was it estimated there were more than 50,000 card-carrying communists. A brief break in antagonism ensued as the Soviet Union joined the Allies in World War II, but there was no indication that the problem had gone away, and the fear took on hysterical and unrealistic proportions. Men and women became suspect over the slightest provocations, loyalty oaths were required, and the persons hurt still carry the scars. But there are few who remember the times or the extent of its affect or the damage done. Many of those greatly harmed by the suspicion, the inquiry, the charges, and the unprovoked anger are still alive, having never fully recovered from the disruption of their lives. The famed "Are you now a communist or have our ever been a member of the communist party?" became the catch phrase of the decade of the '50s.

But, as easy as it is to make such an assumption, the Korean War was not the motivation behind the Red Scare; if anything, the Red Scare was the motivation behind the Korean War. The administration had suffered some significant blows to its anticommunist reputation. George Marshall's failure to reach a compromise in the Chinese Civil War was a major diplomatic loss. The success, and then public display, of Russian spies within the government gave undeserved credence to the atmosphere that allowed the senator from Wisconsin, Joseph McCarthy, to lead the nation into a hysterical witch hunt of clandestine commies. The pressure was on Truman to take some immediate action against this deliberate act of aggression by the international communist conspiracy. In an article in *American Foreign Policy*, Ben Gallup wrote this interesting summary of conditions. What other than the struggle against the communists could have led us to war, he pondered.

"None of the customary reasons for war seemed applicable—in other words, how would the loss of South Korea to North Korea have been of any harm to America?" What was the danger to South Korea, or was the assumption that the domino theory was in action? Was it the belief that a victory in North Korea might set off some sort of Asian rampage, he pondered? Maybe it was the accumulation of North Korean resources that so attracted us. "Whatever they might be there were events in 1949 that helped to instill in America a view of the Soviet Union and a possible great impact of the spread of communism."[8]

This fear gave rise to the principal reason for American involvement in the Korean War. America would not stand idly by as the Soviet

Union forced the spread of Communism around world, he suggested. What was needed, he said, was for America to firmly state that the expansion of communism would not be tolerated, and that any activity beyond a given point would be punished. Something about what was happening in Korea led the United States to feel the need to defend its credibility, but this certainly is less compelling than the fear of communism gaining the momentum necessary to threaten American interests throughout the world. "All told, the American fear of communism, more than an attempt to defend American credibility was the most compelling reason for war."[9]

Current scholarship has given the reasons for the war a new and compelling look, and some suggest a long and prevailing struggle might better explain it. But consider how this atmosphere was tainted by the fear of Moscow and its diabolical efforts to rule the world. Since then the fear has been reconsidered and is more directed at foreign sources, but since we have forgotten our understanding of the full impact of this fear, it became far easier to fall into the same trap once again. To become misguided and frightened by undocumented charges and irrational acts. To have forgotten the role of this fear, not only in America, but in the Western world, is to make light of events and personalities that are waiting in the wings to distract us again.

Unpopular Because We Lost

There is a rather natural assumption found in discussions and printed material about the war. That is that the war became so unpopular with the American people after it was evident that we might well lose it. That does not appear to be the case. The evidence suggests that other than the early weeks of patriotic response, it was never a popular war. Thus to those who suggest it was unpopular because we lost it, there must be the counter consideration that we lost it in part because it was so unpopular.[10] At this date it may not matter, but a clearer picture of the diminishing popularity can explain, at least in part, the lack of interest in the war today.

It does not require much research to determine that the American people, as represented by the press as well as by the government, are still only peripherally interested in what is happening in Korea. This is particularly true of North Korea. Despite the North Korean determination to arm itself with nuclear weapons and to manufacture missiles to transport those weapons to the United States, it has not been of great interest to those who are the intended target. In 2015 only about 54 percent of Americans felt they had anything to fear from the North Koreans. This figure bounces up and down depending a great deal on the Great Leader's rambling. But polls consistently put North Korea below Iraq in the list of dangerous places in the world.[11]

When Truman ordered MacArthur to send men into Korea, 78 percent of the American people approved of the action and believed it was a necessity. Only 15 percent showed any disapproval. As the war progressed, the approval numbers went up and down. In August 1950, 26 percent of Americans felt we should not have gone to the defense of South Korea, but by January of the following year the disapproval rate had risen to 49 percent. By January 1953, disapproval was back at 38 percent.

The one unchangeable fact is that the serviceman never found the war to be popular. Few are recorded as having made an effort to avoid service once enlisted, but there was very little of the mass enlistments as was seen at the beginning of other wars. The individual serviceman was never asked if he agreed with the war or not, but the Information Officer in every outfit came equipped with an explanation as to why they needed to be there. Amazing numbers of veterans will tell you that it was a significant experience, but "I wouldn't give you a dime to do it over again." The veterans' response to why it was so unpopular was almost universally that "no one cared." While a tautology (a work of circular reasoning), it may nevertheless be true. Obviously few cared or it would be remembered, but why did no one care?

The events in Korea itself, as apart from the popularity of the president, are hard to define. But the president was not well liked while in office and much of the bad news from the front was attached to "Mr. Truman's War." He did little to offset this, not being the kind of man who cared too much for his public appeal. His rather cool response, as well as the lack of information he provided the press, led some to believe that his exaggerated optimism was unfounded. In an effort at unity, the chairman of Scripps-Howard suggested to his cartoonists, "No matter what anyone thinks of him he will be the president for the next two years and at a time that I do not know if it would add to the morale of our readers to picture the commander-in-chief as a grinning nincompoop. One might wish for an Eisenhower or a MacArthur, but we have Harry."

The press did not give the war a post-armistice honeymoon as is generally the case. No period of acceptance, or fond memories, or justifications for the nation's behavior. One reason for this, and the situation continued for some time, is that there never were any "redeeming graces." That is to say, the losses of the war were never acknowledged and justified by later and far greater success. There were no offsetting triumphs. The Texans defeated Santa Ana shortly after the loss of the Alamo, and in time Texas became free. The United States Cavalry rounded up and defeated the tribes of the Sioux nation some time after Little Big Horn, and homesteaders were soon on their way to settle in the lands taken away. Americans defeated at Pearl Harbor recovered and destroyed the same Japanese fleet at Midway. General MacArthur returned to Bataan to avenge the death march from which he had escaped, and went on to sign a surrender on the USS *Missouri*. We lost in Korea and we did not take some action to compensate for the loss; we had not returned with any trophies.

Army veteran William St. Clair thought the answer was simple. The war "was not a good investment. We did not recover our costs and no American likes, or will remember, a bad bargain." At one of the few reunions he attended, Wayne Funmaker of the 31 FA commented, "They gave me a couple of medals but I could have used a little something more. What did we do there, or what were the results of our efforts that left us any better off than before we went? Nothing, not even our pride."[12]

The Korean veterans, as they fade away in the clouds of ever new and frightening wars, is very much afraid that the unexamined memory of their call to action is not well understood, and it not to be trusted. If this is the case, then the mission and the accomplishment as well as the hardships and death were very much in vain. For their investment to have been without value does not require that we accept defeat, or that we failed to achieve a goal; rather it is in the fact that we have learned so very little from what happened there, from what we did there.

America Ended World War II Strong

General Hodges, who commanded the occupation in Korea, said that the soldier in Japan had only three things to fear: "Gonorrhea, diarrhea, and Korea." Americans looked on duty in Korea as a hard duty post that served as a punishment post for those who messed up. No one wanted to go. In contrast, their assignment as occupation troops in Japan was easy duty.

Remembering the massive armies of World War II, located all over the world, it is easy to make the primary assumption that as the war was ending the military was strong, intact, and ready for action. This, of course, was not the case. When Truman suddenly decided to fight a ground war in Asia, he bit off far more than the military was ready to chew. As the war ended, the civilian leadership saw the military as a place to balance the budget, and the surrender had hardly been signed when efforts were made to curtail military spending. Nevertheless, the leadership maintained an exaggerated view of American military strength and ability. The truth of the situation was further weakened by an unwise dismissal of the strength and capabilities of the opposing forces. There was little in the military thinking other than survival, and they saw little need for innovation or military action apart from the old rules of engagement and the necessary political constraints on the use of the full arsenal of firepower.

The point is that the American military was not ready to go to war with anyone anyplace; and the fact so many did not understand it at the time of the commitment may help explain why so few understand it today. One early critic of American preparation for war put it fairly simply: the United States military "was in a state of near impotency." It may not have been quite that bad, but it surely was not the healthy, well-dispersed, and finely tuned fighting machine that many assumed.

When World War II ended in 1945, more than 12 million men were under arms, 7.6 million of them overseas. The moment the war ended, Operation Magic Carpet was initiated, and the return of soldiers to the United States was fully underway. By June 1947 the number of men in the military had been reduced by 95 percent. Of these the Army lost 990,000, the Air Force 506,000, the Navy 484,000, and the Marines 92,000. The numbers dropped fast. The Air Force, only recently having gained its independence from the Army, was letting planes rot on the ground in "burial fields," and the Navy was decommissioning or mothballing hundreds of ships. Army equipment rusted where it had been left. When MacArthur tried to land at Wonsan Harbor, he had to revert to Japanese minesweepers and LSTs to clear the path and deliver the troops.

Those who were first sent to Korea were typical occupation troops who lacked heavy equipment, reserve ammunition, mortar tubes, spare parts and working vehicles. Once in Korea they were dealing with roads marked as highways that were impossible to drive on, small hills that turned out to be mountains, and village streams that were in fact impassable. At the time of the roundup of troops for Korea—identified as Operation Flush Out—43 percent of the available troops in Japan were classified four and five, the lowest classification on the army performance scale. Far East Command scraped together every conceivable person—clerks, chaplain's assistants, cooks, mechanics, engineers, even those in the stockades with lesser sentences—and produced a command of 2,430. Some units were made available intact, as was the 8080 Postal Unit. Getting troops to Korea was a massive problem, solved in part by the illegitimate use of Japanese shipping.

The decision to fight in Korea required an immediate rethinking of military policy that had been around since the close of the war. What many meant by being prepared was simply that we had atomic bombs and no one else did. It was quickly apparent that military thinking was operating under the assumption that the presence of nuclear weapons was sufficient to keep us out of war, and to win any war if one became necessary. The big bomber was our salvation.

Then suddenly the big bomber was inadequate. What was needed were conventional weapons. It finally dawned on those facing the problem that the atomic bomb was a political deterrent and not a practical weapon. Korea, this dirty little war in a small insignificant place, dispelled the thesis. The mission in Korea—and certainly the presumed need for troops elsewhere—called for "boots on the ground," and thus began a series of military budgets that established new highs for peacetime commitment. The military requirements imposed by the war, and later by both administrative and public fears, introduced the massive military expenditure as a fact of life for the American society and set in motion an unprecedented growth that continues unabated until today. The loss of domestic progress sacrificed to the demand for more expensive and sophisticated weapons has been an unparalleled tragedy.

The impact of the need and the investment it would require called for a counterbalance to soften the blow. A way was needed to downplay the scope of deployment, the depth of commitment, and the length of time needed to fulfill the requirements. Thus the Korean troops would learn the hard way the need to fight their war in such a way as to avoid frightening or discouraging the domestic community. The fact that the original investment and the potential costs were so well disguised by half-truths and misdirection might well explain why the war was fought and supported by a fewer and fewer representatives of American society. The selling of the war was so well done that Americans had little encouragement to pay close attention to the details of these encounters.

Once the academics got hold of the degree of unpreparedness, they began to make a serious case for it. Now, as might be expected, some reputable historians are making the case that the situation has been exaggerated. How one evaluates the condition of an army is going to depend a good deal on what it is you want that army to do. So for MacArthur, who constantly demanded more troops, there were never enough. On the other hand, if looking at cadre and potential, a smaller army might be sufficient.

One author has reconsidered the situation and did not find it as bad as historians have previously stated. In his well-researched book *Combat Ready* (2000), Thomas Hanson makes a case that the number, disposition, and training level of American troops were being considerably higher than previously demonstrated. While he makes a case, it is not a complete one, and the book ends up basically reaffirming the original question.

Only a Phase of the Cold War

Recently the *Chicago Manual of Style* (8.74) determined that the Cold War was not an event of significant identity or consequence, and therefore it should no longer be capitalized in academic papers. The decision, obviously made by English majors rather than historians, suggests not only a misunderstanding of the Cold War and a limited consideration of the significance of the period, it misleads those attempting to study it. The Cold War, in which the future of the world often hung in the balance, should not now be taken lightly, even if we like to think it is over. The conclusion has often been that the Korean War was the first phase of the Cold War, or perhaps a warm spot in the Cold War. However, the belief that the war in Korea can best be identified as a part of the larger political and social conflict is to give the wrong impression. This is true for two reasons.

The first of these has to do with getting lost in the larger context. When communicating about the nature of an event, there is the need for a distinct name and identity by which to identify its perimeters. Parceling it out makes it harder and harder to identify and thus to acknowledge it as an event in and of itself.

The fact is that attaching the study of the war to a larger field may give the historian, even the politician, some wider perspective. But it is also true that we have never really profited from some of the many lessons that Korea might have taught us. For example, Secretary of the Air Force Thomas Finletter bemoaned that the power of the Korean War to alter air history has never been considered decades after the introduction of nuclear air theory. "Korea was a unique, never-to-be-repeated diversion from the true course of the strategy of Air Power," and thus, he states, needs to be studied in its own right.

General Maxwell Taylor, one-time Commander of U.S. Eighth Army in Korea, complained, "There is no thoroughgoing analysis made of the lessons to be learned from Korea, and later policy makers proceeded to repeat many of the same mistakes." Unfortunately a pattern has developed that was followed in Vietnam, Iraq, and Afghanistan. Wars without declaration and without political consensus, as well as the public resolve to meet specific and changing goals, are in trouble from the start. "These are," wrote James Wright, "ill contested wars. They are dangerous."[13]

Historians of the Korean War are not so much concerned with the question if Korea was a part of, or a corollary to, the Cold War; rather they are concerned that its own significance may be lost in the search for a common denominator. A significance easily lost in the wider and more dramatic search for an international flavor. If it was a part of the whole Cold War scenario, the Korean War was a complex issue with which the United Nations had to successfully deal or lose its credibility. This was just five years after coming into being.[14]

The second has to do with a misunderstanding of the idea of "cold." It has to do with the fact that a situation developed and continued for decades in which warfare was implied but not actualized. An understanding of the Cold War, and any prolonged study of it, must take into account the primary factor that it is in the belligerent behavior that the threat existed, not in any real desire for war. The lessons of the Cold War are found in those solutions other than war which the circumstances provided. Longtime advisor on Soviet affairs George Kennan provided a bit of the wisdom upon which the Cold War operated. The American response to Soviet aggression should be a matter of "long-term, patient, but firm and vigilant containment of Russian expansion."

In neither of these two cases do we profit from identifying a larger, more complex field. In many of today's military and academic histories, the authors seem anxious to expand the identify of these postwar years in such a way as to broaden the explanation. Korea is the part that many believe will serve as the key to understanding the Cold War in its entirety. As reductionists they hope to find parts of the larger consideration to explain the lesser one. They are looking for something about the Cold War that makes the Korean War necessary or unavoidable.

The Cold War started early and with a flourish. The usual dates used to identify the period suggest it began the day World War II came to a conclusion and ended about the time that the Berlin Wall was taken down (1989). It was soon identified as a period of military, economic and political conflict between the Warsaw Pact Countries and NATO. More than a dozen people take credit for coining the phrase. During the war, Iran had served both the United States and the Soviet Union as a significant staging area. When the war was over, the United States pulled out most of its troops. Russia did not, however, and gave evidence that it intended to expand its area of control. The President of the United States send a secret message to the Russian leadership. It sounded very much like an ultimatum. The message said that if the Soviets did not withdraw, the United States would move army and naval forces to the Persian Gulf in preparation for war. The Russian troops left. Nevertheless, the confrontation was dangerous and unpleasant and is seen by many as the first real test of the nation's power. As these and other pressures began to develop, the willingness of the United States and the Soviet Union to maintain the cooperation of World War II began to wane.

Failure in Korea Led to Republican Victory

There is little doubt that the Republicans expressed their disapproval with how the president was dealing with the war in Korea. They found every means possible to turn what should have been a bipartisan issues into a political football. The failure to conclude a victory fed into the harsh anticommunist criticism found on the Hill. After Truman had decided not to run in 1952, the Republican Party opened up full guns against the president's success; "to err is Truman," they shouted, and pointed to a vast array of difficulties that faced the nation. Eventually they were able to break the hold on the presidency for the first time since 1932.

But the somewhat simple affirmation that the war brought about the defeat of the Democratic Party is an unrealistic misunderstanding of the situation. While Truman was a good politician and knew a great deal about dealing with governments, he was also outspoken, brave and even a principled man, all of which meant that during his term of office he made a lot of enemies. Following in the path of a president more loved than understood, Truman brought none of the tools FDR had used to such good service: stature, charisma, an ability to speak and deliver well, plus a Congress that was weak in its opposition.

One of Truman's very first acts as president was to deal with the decision to bomb Japan with nuclear weapons. This was followed up with the loss of China to communism, and the resulting charges of his being "soft on communism." His own political views that combined liberalism and the Democratic Party were ample fodder for attacks of implications that were orchestrated by Congress, especially by McCarthy, that were usually more theatrical than factual. Nevertheless they left the marks of "liberal" and "weak on communist" on Truman and many of his staff. His early support for the Civil Rights Movement, including the integration of the armed services, made him and his Democratic Party a lot of enemies. With every hint of scandal in the White House— whether it be the ridiculous charge that someone had given Bess an old freezer, or evidence of corruption leveled against General McGrath and the Internal Revenue Service, or the outpouring of spy charges by Whittaker Chambers—the integrity of the president was challenged. Truman's loss of popularity, much but not all of it attributed to the war, badly skewed the structure of the Democratic Party and broke its hold on the presidency. His decision not to run again reflected his own understanding of his lost popularity, and the degree to which the firing of MacArthur attributed to his downfall.

Much of the change in command was the result of Eisenhower's wide acceptance. Eisenhower was a military man and that seemed good under the circumstances. His policies were to a rather large degree based on a belief in "situational truth," what most people today call pragmatism. It allowed him to adjust his response to the peculiar needs of the question rather than judging it against some principle.[15]

Some were uneasy. Winston Churchill, who knew Eisenhower well, explained in his memoirs that he was afraid the election of the Republican Eisenhower would greatly increase the chances for global war.[16] The nation seemed to respond to his promise to go to Korea and see what could be done about the war. Though at the time it appeared anticlimactic, the press, at least, thought his later visit was a success. There was more than enough political baggage hanging about the president, and enough hero worship that stuck to Eisenhower, to make the loss of the presidency fairly self-determined, but it does not provide evidence that the war played a major role.

Fought with One Arm Tied Behind Our Back

This is a comforting myth to help generals sleep better at night, but it probably is not true. The long-held myth was primarily the work of MacArthur and his staff and reflected not so much limitation on the fighting of this war, but on the nature of the war to be fought. Korea was not so much a limited war as much as it was an effort to limit the war to the one at hand.

The basis for the complaints of restrictions, and what restrictions involved, got out of hand on more than one occasion when it appeared that the troops were not getting what they needed to fight the war. There is no evidence of an effort on the part of the military or the government to deny much-needed material. There were shortages and distribution screw-ups, of course, but little to no evidence of planned limitations.

Recognizing that the war started with the military in the hole, that significant quantities of supplies were being sent to Europe, that production at home was being interrupted by strikes and walkouts, and that supply sergeants were traditionally absorbing the best equipment before sending the rest to the line, this was a limited war. But the often-repeated stories of limitations reflect another issue, a basic difference of opinion between the commander and his commander-in-chief.

The MacArthur position was fairly simple: the general was psychologically incapable of entertaining the thought that his military strategy was restricted. In a war you needed to have available, and be able to use if necessary, everything you have to win total victory over your enemy. Anything less than that was an appeasement. After more than sixty years of getting his own way, MacArthur could not rest easy with the restrictions imposed on him. He saw a global threat and it required a global response. He affirmed that a communist victory in one sector would be felt in other sectors, and the pressure in Asia would create simultaneous pressure in Europe.

Truman's position was just as simple: it was imperative that this war not be allowed to expand into World War III. MacArthur's behavior in Korea had to be maintained in such a way that it did not upset the delicate balance of understanding under which they operated. Any unexpected or unexplained action might well set off a war with communism, including Moscow. On 11 April 1951, when informing the world of his decision to fire MacArthur, Truman once again reaffirmed the right to be in Korea, but emphasized the need to prevent its expansion into a larger, more deadly conflict.

So what were these limitations that MacArthur could not live with? It is true that the president would not support the general's desire to release the Nationalist Chinese on Taiwan to attack mainland China. It is equally true that Truman refused the general's request that he be allowed to bomb bridges across the Yalu, but then he gave in. The president also took a stand against the military commander's suggestion that he be allow to employ nuclear bombs. He refused, as well, MacArthur's request that he be allowed to bomb select targets in China. The president was not receptive to the general's plan to invade China and take the war to its completion by defeating them. This smarted, as did the failure to get permission to take the air war beyond the Yalu River. To MacArthur this meant he was not able to win, and the only response available to him was to make the public aware of his disagreement.

The term "limited war" sounds like a good excuse, but it is necessary to remember what were the limitations.

Military Integration as a Key to Civil Rights

In 1947 President Truman took an essential step toward ending segregation in the military, and the following year issued Executive Order 9901 that mandated the end to segregation in the armed services. There were to be no exceptions. All the services were slow to act and found all sorts of ways to avoid obedience. It was not for another decade that all units could claim to have complied. While many attempts have been made to acquaint this action and the civil rights movement, it is hard to support. Certainly such an early move was an important step, but it was not a significant key to the improvement in racial relations.

The discrimination faced by African Americans was racial bias, nothing else. In fight after fight, from the American Revolution to World War II, African Americans had participated and proven to be as brave as most men, and on occasion far more so. There was no realistic argument against them as fighting men and women, though the military had "examples" they would pull out when needed.

Black troops began to appear in American combat units when the military discovered it did not have enough men to fill their replacement spots. High casualty rates had emaciated whole units, and replacements coming from the States were not sufficient to meet all the demands. A large source of combat troops was needed and was finally found in the reserves of African Americans serving in noncombat posts all over the world. In time the army, and eventually most of the services, began to integrate replacements into previously all-white units. Their numbers grew as the need grew, and within months most units had a significant number of African Americans on their muster lists.

The presence of racial unity is often given as the war's most obvious domestic success, but there is more there than is acknowledged. One aspect of this discussion that has not received proper attention is found in the basic motivation for military integration. The decision to respond to the Armed Services Integration Act was not motivated by a new sense of racial equality, or even the hope for one, but rather on the very practical reality of body count. The common core for racial equality in the military was pragmatic, the need for replacements with whom to share a common danger. Such a model—"I'd rather play golf next to a black man, than not to play golf at all"—seems to be a crack in the armor of racism and a landmark in the Civil Rights Movement.

The proportion of men and women who served with African Americans and who were still overtly racist is just about the same as those who did not serve. On the one hand, it is not hard to find a vast number of disparaging comments about the black troops. On the other hand, there is generally very little racial identification in letters and photographs, and few such comments preserved in memoirs.

While the degree and the connection is not as yet well established, it is generally believed that the accelerated racial integration within the military in turn aided the movement, but to whatever extent it is true, it was a long time coming.[17]

Conclusion

On the other side of the mountain
[was] another mountain.
—*President Truman's meeting notes 25 June 1950*

The Korean War was most certainly a war for those in Korea, the question that still perplexes many today is whether it was a war for those in America. If it was not a war, why? If it was a war, why so ignored? The Korean War veterans returned with the expectation that the nation had experienced some part of the same war they had been fighting. It was assumed that they had been partners in the endeavor. But that was not so. The populace had not shared this war as they had others. Even World War II veterans were short on empathy.

The war, any war, seems to have lost much of its flavor, as if the taste buds of memory had lost some of their sensitivity. War was not as real as it had once been. Much of the rhetoric remained, but a good deal of the passion was gone. War, we seemed to understand, had finally become more of a tool for political maneuvering than it was the outcome of a crusade, or the pursuit of a moral goal, or the leadership in a matter of principle. In the transition between the "greatest generation" and those in "the shadow of the greatest generation," war had changed; it was understood differently.

One way to note this change is to ask ourselves: was it worth it? This is a valid question even if there is little chance of finding an answer. That is, there are (were) no established or observable goals against which to evaluate our achievement. No way to determine if we had established anything. The final measure of a war, it would seem, is that it achieved the victory that was being sought. But if the goal is simply to draw a line in the sand, or to engage an enemy as evidence of our

162

intentions, or if we wage a war for its own sake, then how do we measure what is accomplished? It's like firing into the air without any interest in where the bullet will land.

In this case the politician, the military leader, the aging civilian, or the veteran might very well provide a different answer. "For me," wrote James Healey on the USS *Irwin*, "the Korean War happened: it was there; I went and I came back. I do feel some modest pride that I was a part of an episode that made the history books. If most Americans don't know or don't care, that's o.k. and to be expected. The Korean War is a part of a the distant past."[1] The primary field commander during the war, Matthew Ridgway, who is often credited with the term "forgotten war," simply asked, "What the hell are we doing in this god-forsaken place?" Rod Serling, in his play *The Rack*, has one of his characters say, "At best Korea seemed to be a inconclusive muddled and bloody affair that we were unable to win and could not afford to lose."[2] For the South Korean veteran (ROKA) who came to live in America, the answer carried with it a sense of guilt. "No," he said, "it was not worth it. But we weren't to blame, were we?"[3] Veteran Lieutenant Gale Bunch spoke for a good many when he said, "Never have American men fought in such a useless war."[4] Military apologist S.L.A. Marshall, a well-known historian at the time, took the middle ground, and claimed it was "right for the wrong reasons."[5] Certainly, in the terminology of those still fighting as the negotiations continued, "It is not worth it to die for a tie." Melinda Pash consolidates her remarks by quoting a veteran who said, "People were calling me a hero and I really wanted to become one, but I was not."[6]

Another factor in evaluating a war is not only identifying what we were seeking, but perhaps equally important, what it cost us. This we truly have not done. Statistics tell us the facts, but they do not tell us the story. If you want to evaluate the costs, it is necessary to visit the wards of the local VA hospital, or look at the checkered lives of husbandless wives and fatherless children, or acknowledge what percentage of our budget still goes to paying off the costs of equipping an army, or the international concerns about America's implied imperialism and its morality. The nation only recently paid off the last benefits awarded during the Spanish-American War; the costs never seem to end.

Conversely, if there are no tools that can help us determine if the war was worth the cost, then at least the question should be, "Could it have been avoided?" A good argument could be made for the belief that a realistic understanding of the situation in Asia might have prevented the original invasion or the Chinese intervention, but most likely not. The roots of that disagreement might well have gone too deep for the war to be avoided. Perhaps if the Truman administration was not already so committed to containment, or if we had held a more realistic comprehension of communism, it might have been prevented. But there is little to suggest this.

A good many current scholars have argued that the lack of foresight among United States policy makers meant the Korean War was inevitable. Some revisionists have dated the beginning of the war as early as the 1930s, while others acknowledge that the personalities, once they became involved, had no other choice. The major events of history might well have been taken over, once again by the contingencies of events.

For the veteran the war's accomplishments, if any, must somehow be balanced against the more than 30,000 dead and 100,000 wounded Americans who invested in it. Perhaps it must account for more than half a century of living in the shadow of more immediate national goals, and a lifetime of wondering why.

For the sake of our nation's soul, we need to remember and acknowledge the memory of those who fought it. To take the time and the effort to reflect upon it. Somehow that has not been happening. Today the restless pace of events, so often driven by data rather than knowledge, has resulted in wars and revolutions and interventions that move so rapidly in and out of existence that few can determine what is happening, only recognizing that things are changing. War has become the default state, and we become engaged in it with very little valid consideration.

It is all moving too fast. For the future of the nation it is important to understand the act of war, and the recording and the memory of those who fought them. One would think that the high cost of our involvement would suggest there is value in our continued considerations of what we paid for.

The other alternative, and the path we seem to have chosen, is to let it go. Perhaps it is better to forget it. Perhaps it is enough to once have known. In today's America there appears to be a great deal of lip-support for the men and women in the armed services. A lot of pregame flag-waving and Veterans Day sales. But a lot of it rings false. There appear to be fewer who know anything about what they faced or what they had accomplished. The value of their contribution is betrayed by a lack of interest in what they had achieved.

Americans have a long history of dealing with the unpleasant and unacceptable in the same way: they have ignored it. The "toilet assumption" maintains: if you can no longer see it, it is gone. Perhaps the war and its impact will, much like MacArthur's old soldier, "just fade away" and time will cleanse us all. Melinda Pasha concludes that the American people did not give the war much attention in the first place, so that it never reached the level of significance that wars once achieved. The soldier's story has become all too common.

Veterans Administration officials tell us that approximately one thousand Korean War veterans die every day. Soon they will all be gone. Then perhaps this haze of unpleasant acknowledgment will go away, and we will forget that we forgot.

Chapter Notes

Acknowledgments

1. *Military Review* 63 (1983): p. 36.
2. Headquarters Far East Command, History Section, Dean Historical Center.
3. Praeger Publishing Company, 2002.
4. Paul M. Edwards, *United Nations Participants in the Korean War* (McFarland, 2013).

Preface

1. Albert Glass and Franklin Jones, *Psychiatry in the United States Army* (GPO, 1954).

Chapter I

1. Shakespeare, *Romeo and Juliet*, 2.1.
2. For an more complete understanding of this idea, check Paul M. Edwards, *To Acknowledge a War: The Korean War in American Memory* (Greenwood, 2000).
3. Michael Pearlman, "Korea: Fighting a War While Fearing to Fight One: Specter of Escalation in Management," p. 389. Unpublished manuscript in the possession of the author.
4. As of August 1999 the *New York Times* was still referring to the war as a "conflict." Robert Athey, *The Retreads* (Xlibris, 1998), p. 342.
5. Jack Tolbert, November 2011 speech at the National California Cemetery dedication. "I could never understand why they called it a conflict. It was as much of a war as I'd ever seen." Korean War Educator, www.koreanwar-educator.org.

Chapter II

1. Many of those who suffered from PTSS as the result of participation in more than one war, often became confused in a time loop, speaking of jungle heat and mountain cold in the same memories.
2. Jon Robinson, "Depression on Quality of Life in Male Combat Veterans," November 10, 2015. www.sgrongpointlaw/com/5206/new-ptsd-depression-and-quality-of-life.

3. Michael J. Davidson, "Post-Traumatic Stress Disorder: A Controversial Defense for Veterans of a Controversial War," *William and Mary* 3, No. 29 (1998): pp. 415–418.

4. For more information on war service anxiety (PTSS) among Korean Veterans, check Julian R. Ikin and R.S. Malcom, "Anxiety Post Traumatic Stress Disorder and Depression in Korean War Veterans 50 Years After the War," *British Journal of Psychiatry* 190, pp. 475–483. This is one of the few studies available and is primarily directed toward Australian veterans.

5. The veteran's appreciation for many of these events is somewhat dampened by the knowledge that the Department of Defense pays the sports teams for the "costs of such activities."

6. Feeling expressed to the author by Dwight G. Gunwels, a Korean veteran considering the lack of VA services available in rural areas.

Chapter III

1. In philosophy, it is the study of how we know what we think we know.

2. KMAG, a small American military advisory force left behind to aid in the development of a South Korean armed forces.

3. John H. Ohly, "Steps in United States Military Activities and Aid to the Republic of Korea," 25 June 1950,Truman Papers, Records of the Joint Chiefs of Staff.

4. Alan Millett, *The Korean War* (Potomac Press, 2007), p. 41.

5. James I. Matray, *The Reluctant Crusade: American Foreign Policy in Korea, 1910–1950* (University of Hawaii Press, 1985), first 60 pages.

6. Bruce Cumings, *The Korean War: A History* (Modern Library Reprints, 2011), p. 17.

7. My reconstruction of these views is greatly dependent on James I. Matray (*ibid.*), and William Stueck. *The Korean War in World History* (Princeton University Press), p. 66.

8. *Ibid.*, p. 3.

9. *Ibid.*, p. 113.

10. Shu Zhang, *Mao's Military Romanticism: China and the Korean War, 1950–1953* (University of Kansas Press, 1955), p. 3.

11. *Ibid.*, p. 10.

12. Harry Truman, *Memoirs: Year of Decisions 1946* (Koneck Associates, 1999), pp. 59–60.

13. Joseph Goulden, *The Untold Story of the Korean War* (McGraw-Hill, 1982), p. 315.

14. Stueck, p. 113.

15. Stueck, pp. 134–136.

16. James Stokesbury, *A Short History of the Korean War* (William Morrow, 1988), p. 35; Michael Varhola, *Fire & Ice: The Korean War 1950–1953* (Savas, 2000), p. 208; Stueck, p. 136.

17. Tom G. Jelson, "CIA Files Saw U.S. Blindsided by Korean War," National Public Radio, Morning Edition, June 25, 2010.

18. Bruce Cumings, *The Roaring of the Cataract, 1947–1950* (Princeton University Press, 1990).

19. Stephen Lendman, "America's War on North Korea," *Dogma and Geopolitics* (April 2013): pp. 2–13.

20. *Ibid.*

21. The above comments on Stone and Cumings reflects a series of letters

between Korean War scholars that are available from the University of Chicago, www. nybooks.com/article/2007/11/22/the-korean-war-exchange.

22. James Perloff, "Report on the Power of Conspiracies," *The Shadow of Power* (Western Island, 1988).

23. The tone of the president's speech at the dedication of the Korean War Memorial emphasizes this idea.

24. President William Clinton, Dedication of the Korean War Veterans Memorial, July 27, 1995.

25. Operation Everready (1952) was designed to overthrow the South Korean president if he went too far afield of UN policy.

26. Stokesbury; I.F. Stone, *The Hidden History of the Korean War* (Review Press, 1969); T.R. Fehrenbach, *This Kind of War: The Classic Korean War History* (Brassey, 1963).

27. Wallace Carroll, "Review of Dean Acheson Report on Twelve Years of War and Cold War," *New York Times*, October 12, 1969, pp. 1–6.

28. NARA. government/education.

29. William Manchester, *American Caesar: Douglas MacArthur 1880–1964* (Little, Brown, 1998), p. 672.

30. "The Soldier from Independence, Missouri," VFW, April 7, 2007.

31. Several historians have come down on the side of the constitutional controversy, believing that the degree of insubordination was not as disconcerting to the president as was the challenge to the Constitution. This author had a change of heart once convinced by Mike Pearlman and others that the policy issue was larger than either obedience, or civilian control. Paul M. Edwards, *To Acknowledge a War.*

32. May 15, 1951, Armed Forces Committee, Congress, 82nd, 1 session, part 2, p. 732.

33. Anna Whitman, *Diary*, December 4, 1954; Brenda Williams, "McChrystal," Truman: Lessons from History,

34. *Ibid.*, p. 123. Anna Whitman was Eisenhower's personal secretary for about eight years.

35. James E. Schnable, "Joint Chiefs of Staff and the Relief of General Douglas MacArthur," in Stanley Sandler, *The Korean War: An Encyclopedia* (Garland, 1995), p. 156.

36. While dozens of books have been written about General MacArthur, it is not clear if we have caught the full story of this man. We do not understand some of his actions for we do not understand him. Someone suggested he was a "practical mystic." For example, MacArthur maintained that "there is no substitute for victory," having borrowed both the words and the implications from Aristotle. But it is necessary for us to remember that neither of these two men considered victory the ultimate goal of involvement. A closer look considers that winning, like everything else, is subservient to political and ethical values. As such, MacArthur saw it as legitimate (ethically acceptable) to ask his soldiers to die in order to obtain a value rather than a victory.

37. Jelson, NPR Morning Edition.

38. *Ibid.*

39. Ben S. Malcom, *White Tigers: My Secret War in North Korea* (Brassey, 1996). For one of the more outlandish accounts, see Operation Broken Arrow.

40. The Combat Infantryman's Badge (CIB) was awarded only to soldiers who had spent active duty time in combat. The army did not think Malcom of the CIA met this qualification.

41. Michael Haas, *In the Devil's Shadow* (Naval Institute Press, 2000).

42. Victor Marchen and John Mark, *The CIA and the Cult of Intelligence* (Alfred Knopf, 1974).

43. As quoted in Paul M. Edwards, *The Korean War: American Soldiers' Lives* (Greenwood Press, 2006).

44. Notes from author's conversation with Roger O'Mallory at the Center for the Study of the Korean War.

45. Maggie Higgins, *War in Korea: The Report of a Woman War Correspondent* (Doubleday, 1951).

46. See interview with Melinda Pash conducted by Richard Ernsberger in *American History Magazine*, March 3, 2014.

47. Sandler Staley. *The Korean War: An Encyclopedia* (Garland, 1995). In March 1952 the Soviet Union reaffirmed the charges and demanded an investigation by the United Nations Disarmament Commission, while the American CIA reported that most non-communists did not take the charges seriously. Albert E. Cowdrey, "Germ Warfare and Public Health in the Korean Conflict," *Journal of the History of Medicine and Allied Sciences* (April 19, 1984).

48. Stephen Endicott and Edward Hagerman, *The United States and Biological Warfare: Secrets of the Early Cold War and Korea* (Indiana University Press, 1999).

49. Julian Ryall, *The Telegraph*, June 10, 2000.

50. Jonathan Soffer, *General Matthew Ridgway: From Progressivism to Reganism 1895–1998* (Construction, 1998), p. 118.

51. Kathryn Weathersby, "To Attack or Not to Attack," *Wilson Center Bulletin* 5; "New Russian Document on the Korean War," *Wilson Center Bulletin* 6–7.

52. Kathryn Weathersby, "Deceiving the Deceivers: Moscow, Beijing, Pyongyang, and the Allegations of Bacteriological Weapons Use in Korea," *Wilson Center Bulletin*, 1.

53. No conspiracy implied here. One wonders what the renewed interest is among academics and why the talks were allowed to go on so long.

54. James Matray, "Villains Again: The United States and the Korean Armistice Talks," *Diplomatic History* 16 (1992): p. 119.

55. *Ibid.*, p. 477.

Chapter IV

1. John Schultz, Korean veteran, in a letter to the author, October 1, 1984.

2. Billy Rae Fellow, CSKW, R-A1907

3. Those involved include President Dwight Eisenhower. His involvement is discussed earlier.

4. For a clearer picture, see the United States Senate Select Committee on POW/MIA, 1992.

5. Weathersby looks at Stalin's death as critical to the signing of the armistice. Chen argues that Mao, who believed that that China was in a strong military position, was in little hurry to pull out. Stalin saw no real advantage in ending the war, and until his death he exercised a strong influence in continuing it. He apparently was aware of the forthcoming election in the U.S. and believed there would be a change in direction then. The short amount of time that passed between the death of the Soviet dictator and the Chinese intervention in the armistice makes it hard to believe they were not closely related.

6. William Broyules, Jr., "Why Men Love War," *Esquire* (November 1984).

7. His comment was about a later war, but it applies here just as well.

8. Gaines Foster, "Coming to Terms with Defeat: Post-Vietnam America and the Post–Civil War South," *VQR* (Winter 1990).

Chapter V

1. "The Marines had to fight their way out of the Chosin Reservoir," T.R. Fehrenbach, *This Kind of War: A Study in Unpreparedness* (Brassey's, 1963), p. 1963.
2. Faris Kirtland, "Soldiers and Marines at Chosin Reservoir: Criteria for Assignment in Combat Command," *Armed Forces and Society* (Winter 1955): p. 257.
3. *Ibid.*
4. Vahola, p. 155.
5. Stueck, 15 September 1950. The Marines lost 22 killed and 174 wounded.
6. He did recommend, and received, unit citations for the Marines involved. It was several decades before the Army units were so recognized.
7. See Mike Fisher in Stanley Sandler, *The Korean War: An Encyclopedia* (Garland Press, 1999).
8. The expansion of the Corps was awesome, going from fewer than 75,000 in 1950 to 216,000 in 1953. Seventy-five percent of the Marines who landed at Inchon were reservists.
9. The casualties at Wolmi-do on the first day of battle were something like 19. The casualty numbers are misleading since historians have decided to include Inchon with the Battle for Seoul, the latter of which was a desperate struggle.
10. Gould, p.192.
11. Most accounts of the landing at Inchon are dependent in some way on Appleman, whose official history is valuable if somewhat bombastic. Roy Appleman, *Escaping the Trap: The United States Army X Corps in Northwest Korea* (Naval Institute Press, 1990).
12. Don Boose, "Over the Beach: U.S. Army Amphibious Operations in the Korean War," Combat Studies Institute, Leavenworth, 2008.
13. In 1871 more than 2000 sailors and marines landed at Inchon in an effort to open Korea to American trade. The invasion was successful.
14. O. Herbert and James T. Wooten, *Soldier* (Dell, 1973), p. 533.
15. A look at several accounts of the Inchon landing indicates much of the same information, and occasionally familiar wording, in Appleman.
16. Clay Blair, *The Forgotten War* (New York Times Books, 1987), p. 451.
17. http://www.doureios.com/magazine/TurksinKorea.html.
18. James Edward Smith, bloc (April 11, 2009).
19. "POWs Left in Korea Troubled Eisenhower Administration," *Kansas City Star*, Sept. 18, 1996. The *New York Times*, on Oct. 4, 1996, released a news article titled "Other Views POWs Written Off. Evidence is mounting that a substantial number of American prisoners of war were not released at the conclusion of the Korean Conflict."
20. Some question this response as the nation was already at war.
21. Newly released documents from the Dwight D. Eisenhower Presidential Library. Joseph H. Douglas, Jr., *Betrayed: The Story of Missing American POWs* (Oxford University Press, 2002).
22. *Ibid.*, p. 3
23. Sandler, p. 255.
24. John Zimmerles and Mark Sauter, *American Trophies: How American POWs Were Surrendered to North Korea, China, and Russia by Washington's Cynical Attitude* (Createpress, 2013).

Chapter VI

1. As a part of understanding their attitude, it is interesting to note that a veteran who served in both wars is more likely to identify with World War II and often makes it a point not to even mention Korea.

2. Ronnie Breakwater, speaking at a Korean Veterans Association meeting Overland Park, Kansas, in July 2013.

3. Phrase used originally for those politicians who ran for office on their war records in the Civil War. Later used in post–World War I and II.

4. Matthew Ridgway, *The Korean War: We Met the Challenge* (Doubleday, 1967), p. 10.

5. Notes of interviews, CSKJ R- 0007.

6. It is hardly more than an intuitive impression, but it is nevertheless interesting to note how often it comes up. Some observers have pointed out that the faces of those identified during the war are different from previous and later wars. What is suggested is an attitude of absence that is mirrored in the faces of those involved in Korea. Photographs that appear in magazines like *Yank* and *Life* for both Korea and World War II reveal a contrast between the often exhausted but positive faces of the World War II soldier and the bedraggled absent look on the faces of the Korean soldier. The strange look suggests he is affected by his environment, but in some manner is separated from the reality of it.

7. Pash, p. 11.

8. A reading of dozens of memoirs makes it appear reasonable that what some of these men are remembering is the feeling of the friendship, not so much identifying with the individual.

9. Obviously no statistics are available on such a point, but hundreds of postwar letters, and the comments made on the back of old photographs, suggest that most comrades lost touch and thus connection with each other within six month of their release.

10. Unpublished incomplete manuscript, marked *My Time*, CSKW R-AS 18665.

Chapter VII

1. The Society for International Law tells us that of the last 4000 years only 286 have been without a war. How can we speak of geography, or social sciences, or literature, or music, or anything in the national character, and not consider the role of war? How can we remember the history of a nation and leave out its wars?

2. See later discussions on the relevance of the discipline of history.

Chapter VIII

1. Lewis Carlson explains there were between 250 and 758 involved, and that 74 to 85 were killed.

2. Stueck, p. 79.

3. Brassey's, 1963.

4. Maggie Higgins, *The War in Korea: A Report of a Woman Combat Correspondent* (Doubleday, 1951). The worst example of this is John Toland's *In Mortal Combat: Korea 1950–1953* (Chicago University Press, 1965), in which the author creates dialogue for the main characters to speak without any consideration of how he might have such information.

5. Phillip Knightley, *The First Casualty: From Crimea to Vietnam, The War Correspondent as Hero* (Harcourt Brace Jovanovich, 1975), p. 338.

6. There were fifty-four correspondents killed in World War II.

7. Lisa Rose, *The Cold War Comes to Main Street: America in 1950* (University of Kansas Press, 1999), p. 226.

8. Affirmed by the 1952 announcement by the military that they were "reducing restrictions" and would no longer deny publication of information on the grounds the information might upset the American public.

9. July 25, 1953.

10. She was Anna Wallis Suh from Arkansas, who had gone to Korea as a missionary.

11. The Korean War Educator has a listing of all *Life Magazine* articles and photographs published during the Korean War.

12. "TV News and the Korean War." C:Users/Dad/Appdata/Local/Temp/9FA4 MayQ.htm.

13. Edward H. Carr, *What Is History?* (Vintage Press, 1967), p. 38.

14. "From the first moments of awareness it was not an experience but an encounter, not an event but an intervention. The cold imprisoned you and you no longer acted independently but rather as a vastly vulnerable soul whose every consideration was to delay the solidification of its being. Essence is focused on holding back the terrible sensation of hostile penetration. Soon the cold could only be defined by absence." Sergeant Jay Sparrow, writing some sixty years later. Almost every history written about the war mentions the cold, and include it in the description of the present, but rarely consider it as a changing impact of the conduct of the war. CSKW R-A11X2.

15. In philosophy, this phenomenon is identified as "experimental philosophy."

16. Susan Matt, *American Heritage* (August 2016): p. 23.

17. J.H. Flaskerud and B.J. Winslow, *Conceptualizing Vulnerability in Populations in Nursing Research* (University of Maryland, 1998). Dozens of narrative histories of the war have been published in the last two decades or so, but none of them have taken seriously the impact of prostitution and rape, or either the military of the civilians involved.

18. In a nutshell, he suggests that looking at something changes the way it appears. Another possibility, however, is that the cause is not found in the effect but often in the natural state. The rats in the cage who die of cancer after being fed coffee may not be sickened by the coffee but by being in a cage.

19. A significant danger of reductionism, and one that is evidenced in many of the narrative histories of the Korean War, is that if the total reflects the sum of the parts, sooner or later various parts have to be identified, or adjusted, to provide the total reflection that he historian seeks.

20. James Van der Dussen, *The Idea of History* (Oxford University Press, 1944), p. 54.

21. Dwight Carter, "Carpet-bombing Falsehoods About a War That Is Little Understood," *New York Times*, July 21, 2010.

22. Notes taken by the author at a annual meeting of the Western History Association in 1966 after a brief conversation with the star.

23. Robert Altman himself was apparently not all that impressed with the film, calling it "really terrible." Director/Commentary, DVD, *M*A*S*H*, Twentieth Century–Fox, 2004.

24. It is interesting, if not deliberate, that General Douglas MacArthur and President Syngman Rhee rarely appear in films. The same is true to a lesser degree of other well-known generals and figures. In films they are generally referred to by name, or silhouette, but few full views.

25. Christopher W. Wilson, *American Historian* (August 2016): p. 12.

26. Produced by the Rev. Sun Myung Moon's Unification Church, who believed the landing was an act of God. The movie was voted by several critics as the worst film ever made.

27. The difficulty of trying to escape while a prisoner in a land as foreign to our people as was Asia, was multiplied by the fact that one could not get lost in the crowd, The U.S. POW had the same problem in Japan during World War II.

28. See commentary on the Rambo films.

29. "The food at the restaurant," he warned us, "was awful, but at least there was a lot of it."

30. It seemed strange that English, which has a number of words to describe love, has so few to describe pain. Particularly since it is arguable that there is more pain than love in the world. Somehow the medical profession has accomplished little when it replaced the traditional marks of mild, moderate, and severe with picking a number between one and ten.

31. Joanna Bourke, "Pain through the Prism of War," *BBC History Magazine* 15, #6: pp. 37–41.

32. Lester H. Brune, *The Korean War: Handbook of the Literature and Research* (Greenwood Press, 1996), pp. 42–427.

33. Pickle Partners Publishing, 2015.

34. The original intention had been to use this title for the film *Battle Circus*, with Humphrey Bogart, that told a silly but somehow more realistic tale of the mobile units.

35. Yvonne Klein as quoted in Axelsson, p. 208.

36. The exception to this is the vast amount of amateur poetry published by the Hospitalized Veterans Writing Project that encourages poetry as a tool in recovery.

37. Paul M. Edwards, *The Hermit Kingdom* (Center for the Study of the Korean War, 1995), p. x.

38. Famous Korean War Poems, poetrysout.com/famous/poetry'/korean_war.

39. There is a chicken/egg problem here. Did publishers not publish Korean War materials because there was so little written, or was there so little written because publisher were reluctant to publish it?

40. Matthew Ridgway, *The Korean War* (Da Capo Press, 1986), p. 88.

41. Not without some sense of humor on the subject, the authors followed up with "Dear Joan," in which the soldier replied, "That's okay, I've fallen in love with your sister."

42. In the photographic collection of the Center for the Study of the Korean War, well over a fifth of the snapshots are of Asians identified as "babysans."

43. It is hardly a reliable source, but it is indicative of the problem: the Wikipedia entry for "The War Artist" does not mention Korea, jumping from World War II to Vietnam.

44. In such an understanding, the idea of a Museum of Modern Art is a paradox, and postmodernism an impossibility.

45. It was about this time that so many counties were added to local government and many were named after the Hero of New Orleans. Over the years they have built numerous statues of the general in commemoration of the county, not the war.

46. A resurgence of the 19th-century laissez faire economic system that is reflected in economic liberalism and the private-sector takeover of most services.

47. The Korean War has so few unique artifacts that reflect its character that this practice is even more widely used.

48. Smithsonian Institution, 2004, p. 4.

49. Gary Burnett, veteran, suggested that it looked as if the curator had asked his staff, "Can you include the Korean War in this display without really including it?"

50. It is very interesting that there is not even a map that locates Korea in relation to the rest of the world.

Chapter IX

1. We did not read their books—not Hitler's, nor Mussolini's, and apparently not Mao's—or we might have been a little more cautious about a negotiated peace. Of course, the Chinese did not give up all its prisoners of war.
2. The five-volume detailed history of the war produced by South Korea is about all that is available. Few American scholars are qualified for a study of Korea.
3. Paul M. Edwards, *United Nations Participants in the Korean War* (McFarland, 2013), p. 13.
4. Canada, Australia, New Zealand, United Kingdom, India, and even Ireland made major contributions.
5. Korean War Educator, www/koreanwar-educator.org.
6. The USS *Pueblo*, an American warship, was boarded and taken by elements of the North Korean Navy on January 23, 1968. The ship now serves as a museum in Korea. The crew was held as hostages for more than a year. The United States finally apologized.
7. Kathryn Weathersby.
8. Ben Gallup, "Kommunism, Kredibility and the Korean War," identified as "Paper the First," *American Foreign Policy*. Truman Papers.
9. *Ibid.*
10. Darian Cobb, "An Unnecessary Risk." Unpublished paper in possession of the Center for the Study of the Korean War.
11. Age seems to have a great deal to do with this. A recent poll (2015) suggests that more than 75 percent of Americans who are over the age of 55 disapprove of the war and continue to see North Korea as a threat.
12. St. Clair and Funmaker, CSKW, R-! 1300 Miscellaneous.
13. See Andrew Bacevick, "Thank You for Your Service, Sort Of," a review of James Wright's *Those Who Have Borne the Battle: A History of America's Wars and Those Who Fought Them* (Public Relations Press, 2012).
14. Logistically, when the Korean War broke out, "it heated up the Cold War, thus the war was no longer cold and thus misnamed and probably misunderstood." Comment by Scottish historian William Kerr.
15. Martin Meshuane, *Dwight D. Eisenhower: Strategic Communicator* (Greenwood Press, 1999), p. 11.
16. Michael Hickey, *The Korean War: The West Confronts Communism* (John Murray Press, 1999), p. 317.
17. Korean War Educator, www/koreanwar-educator.org.

Conclusion

1. James Healey on board the USS *Irwin* (DD 791) Ships Article 831.
2. *The Rack*, MGM, 1956.
3. Healey on board the USS *Irwin*.
4. Comments in the *United News Sentinel*.
5. S.L.A. Marshall, in "Ratio of Fire," *Royal United Services Institute of Defense* 133, p. 1989.
6. Pash, p. 302, n. 39.

Bibliography

Primary Sources

After Action Reports (miscellaneous and scattered). Center for the Study of the Korean War Correspondence File, Veterans, Manuscript letters.

Incidental Files, National Archives, College Park, Maryland. There are 1.6 million pages of captured North Korean documents housed there, most of which are available for use.

"Korean War." General Files, Eisenhower Presidential Library and Museum, Acheson, Kansas.

"Korean War Oral History Project." U.S. Eighth Army Historical Office, Eighth Army Command, Seoul, Korea, 1988 (by mail).

Letter from Chief of Staff, United States Air Force to Director Central Intelligence, 16 March 1954. Truman Presidential Museum and Library, Independence, Missouri.

Oral History/Memoirs. Record Group A 001-1900. Center for the Study of the Korean War (CSKW), Independence, Missouri.

"Pink Files." Papers dealing with the Korean War. Harry S. Truman Presidential Library and Museum, Independence, Missouri, located at the Center for the Study of the Korean War, Independence, Missouri.

Secondary Sources

Acheson, Dean. *Present at the Creation: My Years at the State Department*. Norton, 1969.

Adams, Julia, Elisabeth Clements, and A. Orloff. *Remaking Modernity: Politics, History and Sociology*. Duke University Press, 2005.

Alexander, Bevin. *The First War We Lost*. Hippocrates Books, 1991.

Appleman, Roy. *Escaping the Trap: United States Army X Corps in Northwest Korea*. United States Naval Institute Press, 1990.

Athey, Robert Leland. *The Retreads*. Xlibris Corporation, 1998.

Axelsson, Arne. *Restrained Response: American Novels of the Cold War and Korea, 1945–1962*. Greenwood Press, 1990.

Blair, Clay. *The Forgotten War*. New York Times Book, 1987.

Boehem, Scott. "Privatizing Public Memory: The Price of Patriotic Philanthropy and the Post-9/11 Politics of Display." *American Quarterly* 58: pp. 1147–1166.

Bolton, Richard Russell. "Portrayal of the Garrison Military in American Fiction 1946–1970." Ph. D. diss., Washington State University, 1972.

Boose, Donald W., Jr. "Perspectives on the Korean War." *Parameters* (Summer 2002): pp. 118–123.

Bourke, Joann. "Bodily Pain, Combat, and the Politics of Memories: Between the American Civil War and the War in Vietnam." *Histoire Sociale* 46 (91), pp. 43–61.

_____. The Story of Pain: From Prayer to Painkillers. Oxford University Press, 2014.

Casey, Steven. "Selling the Korean War: Propaganda, Politics, and Public Opinion in the United States, 1950–1953." *Journal of Social History* 44 (Summer 2011).

Coakley, R.W., P.I. Scheips, and E.J. Wright, with G. Horne. "Antiwar Sentiments in the Korean War 1950–1953." In Stanley Sandler, *The Korean War: An Encyclopedia*. Garland Publishing, 1955.

Collins, Lawton J. *War in Peacetime: The History and Lessons of Korea*. Houghton Mifflin, 1969.

Cumings, Bruce. *The Roaring of the Cataract, 1947–1950*. 2 vols. Princeton University Press, 1990.

Edwards, Paul M. *The Korean War: American Soldiers' Lives*. Greenwood, 2006.

_____. To Acknowledge a War: The Korean War in American Memory. Praeger, 2000.

Ehrhart, William, and Philip Jason. *Retrieving Bones: Stories and Poems of the Korean War*, Greenwood Press, 1996.

Fallows, James. "The Tragedy of the American Military." *Atlantic* (January 2015): p. 73.

Foot, Rosemary. *The Wrong War: American Policy and the Dimensions of the Korean Conflict, 1950–1953*. Cornell University Press, 1985.

Footitt, Hilary. "Introduction Languages and the Military: Alliances, Occupation and Peace Building." *Language and the Military*. Palgrave, Rowe, UK, 2012.

Forslund, Catherine. "Worth a Thousand Words: Editorial Images of the Korean War." *Journal of Conflict Studies* 22 (Spring 2002).

Herz, Peggy. *All About M*A*S*H*. Scholastic Book Services, 1975.

Hughes, Chris. *War Is the Force That Gives Us Meaning*. Public Affairs, 2002.

Hurh, Won Moo. *"I Will Shoot You from a Loving Heart": The Memoirs of a South Korean Officer of the Korean War*. McFarland, 2011.

James, D. Clayton. "Command Crisis: MacArthur and the Korean War." Harmon Memorial Lecture #24. November 12, 1981.

_____. "MacArthur and the Chinese Communist Intervention in the Korean War, September–December 1950." *Naval Command and Heritage Center*, January 2014.

Junger, Sabastian. *Tribe: On Homecoming and Belonging*. Twelve, 2016.

Kabatchnick, Craig M. "PTSD and Its Effects on Elderly, Minority, and Female Veterans of All Wars." *Marquette Elder's Advisor* 10, No. 2 (Spring 2009).

Kardiner, Abram, and Herbert Spiegel. *War Stress and Neurotic Illness*. Paul Oeger, 1947.

Keene, Judith. "Lost to Public Commemoration: American Veterans of the Korean War." *Journal of Social History* 44 (Summer 2011).

Kim, Daniel Y. "National Technologies of Cultural Memory and the Korean War: Militarism and Neo-Liberalism in the Price of Freedom and the War Memorials of Korea." *Cross Current: East Asian History and Culture Review* (March 2015).

Kolb, Richard K. "Korea's Invisible Veterans' Return to an Ambivalent America." *Veterans of Foreign Wars*, November 1977.

Logtt, J. "Keepers of History." *Penn State Research* 23, No. 2 (2002).

Matray, James I. "Exposing Myths of the Forgotten War." Part 2. *Prologue* 34 (Summer 2002).

_____. "Villain Again: The United States and the Korean Armistice Talks." *Diplomatic History* 16 (1992): p. 473.

Nigel, Thomas, Peter Abbot, and Mike Chandler. *The Korean War 1950–1953*. Osprey, 1986.

Pash, Melinda L. *In the Shadow of the Greatest Generation*. New York University Press, 2012.

Pearlman, Michael. "Korea: Fighting a War While Fearing to Fight One, Specter of Escalation in Management." Unpublished manuscript in possession of the author.

Peters, Richard, and Xiaobing Li. *Voices from the Korean War: Personal Stories of American, Korean and Chinese Soldiers*. University of Kentucky Press, 2005.

Richardson, Bill, and Kevin Mauer. *Valley of Death: Memoirs of the Korean War*. Berkley Group, 2010.

Schnurr, Paula. "PTSD and Combat Related Psychiatric Symptoms in Older Veterans." *PTSD Research Quarterly* 2, No. 1 (Winter 1991).

Scott, Cord A. *Comics and Conflict: Patriotism and Propaganda from World War II Through Operation Iraqi Freedom*. United States Naval Institute Press, 2014.

Slator, Jay. *Under Fire: A Century of War Movies*. Ian Allan, 2009.

Steele, Bruce. "Historians Debunk Some Popular Myths About the War." University of Pittsburgh, *University Times* 32, No. 21 (June 22, 2000).

Stokesbury, James L. *A Short History of the Korean War*. William S. Morrow, 1988.

Stueck, William. *The Korean War in International History*. Princeton University Press, 1994.

_____. "Revisionism and the Korean War." *The Journal of Conflict Studies* (Spring 2002).

Sturken, Maritra. "The Aesthetics of Absence: Rebuilding Ground Zero." *American Ethnologist* 31, No. 3: p. 311.

Styron, William. "If You Write for Television." *New Republic* 140, No. 14/2316 (1950).

Sutker, P.B., D.K. Winstead, and Z.H. Galin. "Cognitive Defects and Psychopathology Among Former Prisoners of War and Combat Veterans of the Korean Conflict." *American Journal of Psychiatry* 148: pp. 67–72.

Suzuki, Tessa Morris. "Post War Warriors: Japanese Combatants in the Korean War." *Japanese Forum*, 2004.

Vandon, Major Jenerett. "The Forgotten DMZ." *The Korean War Project*.

Varhola, Michael J. *Fire & Ice: The Korean War 1950–1953*. Savas, 2000.

Vogel, Steve. "50 Years Later, An Army Force Gets Its Due." *Washington Post*, December 11, 2000.

Xiaoyuan Liu. "Review of Shu Zhang *Mao's Military Romanticism: China and the Korean War, 1950–1953*." University of Kansas Press, 1955; published in History-Diplomatic, June 1997.

Zhang, Shu. *Mao's Military Romanticism: China and the Korean War, 1950–1953*. University of Kansas Press, 1955; published in History-Diplomatic, June 1997.

Zimerlee, John, and Mark Sauter. *American Trophies: How American POWs Were Surrendered to North Korea, China, and Russia by Washington's Cynical Attitude*. Createpress, 2013.

Electronic Sources

Cowley, Robert. "*What If? The World's Foremost Military Historians Imagine What Might Have Been*." www.thefreelibrary.com/what+if.

Ehrenreich, Barbara. "The Personal is Political." margieadam.com/action/ehrenreich.htm.

Bibliography

Haan, Phil de. "50 Years and Counting: The Impact of the Korean War on the Peninsula." Korean War Educator. www/koreanwar-educator.org.

Loyola, Mario. "The Korean War and the Incoherence of U.S. Foreign Policy." http://nationalreview.com/corner/354579.

MacDonald, J. Fred. "Television and the Red Menace: The Video Road to Viet Nam." Users/Dad/AppData/Local/Temp/9FAMAYQ.htm.

Meyer, William P. "Notes from Memoirs by Harry Truman." http://www:iipublishing.com/poliics/sian_wqr/koea_truman_notes.

Robinson, Jon. "New Study: PTSD, Depressing and Quality of Life." http:Strongpoint law./5206 (reviewed October 2016).

"Sixty Years After the Korean War: Veterans Still Suffer Silently." http://broadside.com/sixty-years-after-the-korean-war-veterans—still-suffer-in-silence.

Veterans History/ http: www.theforgotten—victory.org.

Vlassis, Savvas D. "The Turks in Korea: Creating a Myth." www.doureios.com/magazine/Turksinkrea.html.

Index

Chosin 62–65, 67, 79, 107, 113, 132
Christmas 66, 99
Churchill, Winston 158
CIA *see* Central Intelligence Agency
CIB *see* Combat Infantryman's Badge
Civil Rights 147, 157, 160
civilian 3, 13, 32, 35, 37, 46, 75, 80, 81, 83, 85, 86, 89, 90, 91, 100, 120, 152, 163
Clark, General Mark 71
Clinton, President Bill 135, 145
Coast Guard 63
Cold War 54, 55, 97, 133, 137, 138, 144, 145, 151, 155, 156, 175n14
Cole, Nat King 128
combat 130, 131, 154, 160
Combat Infantryman's Badge 41, 169n40
Commander in Chief 26, 144, 159
commemorations 5, 118, 124, 174
Commonwealth 143
communications 66, 132, 137
Communism 3, 9, 20, 22, 23, 25, 30, 36, 39, 44, 56, 57, 101, 102, 115, 122, 138, 147, 148, 149, 157
Communist Party 19, 22, 24, 25, 147, 148
confessions 46
conflict: Korean 1, 3, 5, 8, 10, 21, 59, 74, 110, 128, 137, 147, 167n4; other 2, 7, 11, 20, 34, 53, 83, 91, 95, 156
Congress 8, 29, 61, 63, 72, 79, 81, 110, 135, 157
conscription 74, 84
conspiracy 23, 28–31, 142, 148, 170n53
constitution 36, 168
constitutional controversy 169n31
containment 136, 164
contingencies 102, 164
correspondents 67, 97, 100, 172n6
court martial 43
court room 113
cowardliness 36, 45, 54, 115
Crans, Conrad 47
Creel, George 147
Cumings, Bruce 20, 29, 30, 108
Currier, James 1

Dear John letter 129
defeat 42, 44, 56, 65, 68, 97, 154, 157
defectors 113
Defense Department *see Secretary of Defense*
Demarcation Line 145
Demilitarized Zone (DMZ) 141, 144, 146, 179
Democracy 28, 32, 33, 57, 89, 102

Democratic Party 157
Democratic People's Republic of Korea 18, 23, 25, 26, 29, 30, 33, 38–40, 41, 46, 47, 59, 84, 70, 71, 81, 143, 145, 146, 148, 150
Department of Defense *see* Secretary of Defense
diarrhea 152
discharge 73, 113
dissenters 25, 147
A Distant Drum 121
Doll, Jackie 128
Domino, Fats 128
DPRK *see* Democratic People's Republic of Korea
draft dodgers 148
Dulles, Alan 41
Dulles, John Foster 20, 29, 71
Duncan, David 31

Eastwood, Clint 111, 112
education 53, 86, 88, 114, 140
8th Army 52, 62, 64
Eisenhower, Dwight 5, 28, 94, 151, 155
Elsey, George 143
emotional sensitivity 105
empathy 15, 115, 162
enlisted men 5, 45, 123
Enoch, Kenneth 47
epistemology 18
escape 45, 105, 113, 151
ethnic studies 86
Europe (European) 3, 25, 28, 33, 34, 40, 46, 74, 87, 119
evacuation 2, 66

Executive Order #9901 160
"Fallacy of the Misplaced Concreteness" 107
Far East Command 38, 153, 167
Farewell to Arms 124
Fatherland's Liberation War 10
Fehrenbach, T.R. 34, 63, 95
Flaskerud, J.H. 106
Flying Fish Channel 64
Forgotten War 10, 125
Frank, Pat 120
free verse 126
French and Indian Wars 65
Front Line Camera 101
Fulbright, Senator 139
Funmaker, Wayne 83, 151
Fussell's, Paul 126

G-2 (Far East Command) 38
Gallup, Ben 148